Subjects in Poetry

Subjects in Poetry

DANIEL BROWN

Louisiana State University Press
Baton Rouge

Published by Louisiana State University Press
lsupress.org

LSU Press Paperback Original

Designer: Barbara Neely Bourgoyne
Typeface: Calluna

Cover image: iStockPhoto.com/CreatorOfTheVector

Cataloging-in-Publication Data are available from the Library of Congress.

ISBN 978-0-8071-7609-2 (pbk.: alk. paper) — ISBN 978-0-8071-7666-5 (pdf) —
ISBN 978-0-8071-7667-2 (epub)

To Alice van Straalen: my work's best friend

CONTENTS

PREFACE AND ACKNOWLEDGMENTS

The subject of subjects in poetry is like a mountain you're standing at the base of: so huge you can fail to see it unless you look upward. This book is one poet's attempt at a lifting of eyes.

Its first chapter ventures a definition of *subject*—a less straightforward task than it might seem, where poetry is concerned—and applies it to a selection of poems.

Its second chapter is a case for the value of subjects. You'd think such a case wouldn't be needed, but at a time when many poems are subjectless, I wanted to put one on the record.

The third chapter is about working with subjects. It focuses on approaches I've found especially helpful and haven't seen discussed elsewhere. Perhaps they'll prove helpful to others, though I know better than to count on this. (I almost said "Bank on this," but that would bring remuneration into a picture where it couldn't be more out of place.)

This book grew out of a workshop I give on poetic subjects. I first offered it at the Frost Farm Poetry Conference; my thanks to conference director Robert Crawford for letting me debut it there. My thanks as well to Deborah Wieringa for suggesting that I turn the workshop into a book. I'm also grateful to the following early readers of the book for their interest, feedback, and encouragement: Ray and Catherine Bacon, Adam Brown, Susan de Sola, Anne Hammel, David Katz, Mike Levine, Alfred Nicol, William Pritchard, Jan Schreiber, Linda Stern, Jay and Jan Swain, Alice van Straalen, Helen Vendler, and Ann Woodward.

W. S. Merwin, "For the Anniversary of My Death," in *The Essential W. S. Merwin,* edited by Michael Wiegers, copyright © 1967 by W. S. Merwin. Reprinted with the permission of The Permissions Company LLC on behalf of Copper Canyon Press, coppercanyonpress.org.

W. S. Merwin, "For the Anniversary of My Death," in *Selected Poems* (Bloodaxe Books, 2007). Reproduced with permission of Bloodaxe Books. www.bloodaxebooks.com.

"For the Anniversary of My Death" by W. S. Merwin currently collected in *The Second Four Books of Poems.* Copyright © 1960, 1961, 1962, 1963, 1964, 1965, 1966, 1967, 1968, 1969, 1970, 1971, 1972, 1973, 1993 by W. S. Merwin, used by permission of The Wylie Agency LLC.

Excerpt from "The Colonel" in *The Country Between Us* by Carolyn Forché. Copyright © 1981 by Carolyn Forché. Used by permission of HarperCollins Publishers and the Clegg Agency.

"This Is Just to Say" by William Carlos Williams, from *The Collected Poems: Volume I, 1909–1939,* copyright © 1938 by New Directions Publishing Corp. Reprinted by permission of New Directions Publishing Corp. and Carcanet Press, Manchester, UK.

"Sappho: Fragment 35" from *Sappho's Lyre: Archaic Lyric and Women Poets of Ancient Greece,* translated by Diane J. Rayor, published by the University of California Press. Copyright © 1991 by The Regents of the University of California.

"A Wonderful Guy" from *South Pacific.* Lyrics by Oscar Hammerstein II. Music by Richard Rodgers. Copyright © 1949 Williamson Music Company c/o Concord Music Publishing. Copyright Renewed. All Rights Reserved. Used by Permission. Reprinted by Permission of Hal Leonard LLC.

Excerpt from "Dogs Who Are Poets Who Are Movie Stars" by David Kirby is reproduced by permission of LSU Press.

My poems "A Salmon Speaks," "At Ease," "Deliverance," "The Birth of God," and "Where I Was" first appeared in my book *Taking the Occasion*, published by Ivan R. Dee, copyright © 2008 by Daniel Brown. My poem "His Father's Son" first appeared in *What More?*, published by Orchises Press, copyright © 2015 by Daniel Brown.

Some of the writing in this book has appeared, in different form, in the *Best American Poetry Blog*, *Cortland Review*, *Hopkins Review*, and *PN Review*. I'm grateful to the editors of these publications.

Subjects in Poetry

I

Subject as Something to Say

An online dictionary defines *subject* as "a basic matter of thought, discussion, investigation, etc." This definition is fine for most purposes, but one runs into trouble in applying it to poetry. It works well enough for a poem like, say, Alfred, Lord Tennyson's little classic "The Eagle."

> He clasps the crag with crooked hands;
> Close to the sun in lonely lands,
> Ring'd with the azure world he stands.
>
> The wrinkled sea beneath him crawls;
> He watches from his mountain walls,
> And like a thunderbolt he falls.

The "basic matter" of this poem is, not to put too fine a point on it, an eagle. This subject sits at the poem's center, where it exerts a kind of gravitational attraction on a set of observations that could be said to orbit it.

But what about something like, say, Hamlet's soliloquy? Is its basic matter suicide? Death? The passage is about both of these things—or, to do fuller justice to what's going on in it, about the movement in Hamlet's mind from the former to, and through, the latter. If "The Eagle" can be figured as an orbit, Hamlet's soliloquy can be figured as a journey, from thought to thought.

The figure of a journey can also be applied to narrative poems. Take Ovid's account of the King Midas story. You could say that the subject of this poem is the wages of greed, but I'd call that its theme, not its subject. You could say its subject is King Midas, but where would that leave the Midas *story*? Mightn't the subject of the poem be the plot of this story? (When we're asked what a story "is about," don't we typically respond with a plot summary?) As Hamlet's soliloquy travels from thought to thought, so the Midas story travels from event to event.

In applying the word *subject* to the attractor in an orbital poem and the path of a journeying one, we may be using the same word for insufficiently similar things. As I ponder this possibility, I think of an observation in Robert Frost's essay "The Figure a Poem Makes." He says that the importance of subjects "leaves us back in poetry as merely one more art of having something to say." "Something to say": might *that* serve as a definition of subject? Among other virtues, it would apply to orbiting and journeying poems alike.

A poem can say something in one or more of several ways: by expressing and/or evoking and/or addressing. In this chapter I'll consider each of these ways-of-saying in turn, first defining it and then looking at some poems in which it predominates. I hope to suggest, in the process, the vast range of possible subjects for poems. It can seem as if half the new poems these days are about the death of the poet's parent (if they aren't busy botanizing—as William Carlos Williams didn't *quite* say, "No ideas but in shrubs"). Whereas the poems in this chapter's transhistorical sampler are about all manner of things. As the shaking of a snow globe liberates a flurry of flakes, so a stroll through such a verse gallery may shake up one's idea of the sphere of subjects to where it's milling with possibilities.

SOME POEMS THAT SAY BY EXPRESSING

A poem that says by expressing gives vent to an emotion. Of course, some would say all poems do that. There's even a gold-plated precedent for thinking so: Wordsworth's famous definition of poetry as "the spontaneous overflow of powerful feelings." This definition calls to mind a locution in the title of a poem of his: "Extempore Effusion upon the Death of James Hogg." Some expressive poems effuse, but others (including some canonical ones) don't.

Expressing is probably the way of saying that first comes to mind when one thinks of poetry, but comparatively few poems purely express. (Though there's a huge body of sort-of-poems that do: the lyrics of the countless operatic arias devoted entirely to the expression of emotion, sometimes a very particular emotion, as in "revenge arias" and the like.) Consider, in this connection, one of the oldest known expressive poems, at least in the Western tradition: Sappho's fragment 35. (Only one of her poems has survived in its entirety.) Its subject is an access of passion. Here it is in a translation by Diane Rayor:

> To me it seems
> that man has the fortune of the gods
> whoever sits beside you, and close,
> who listens to you sweetly speaking
> and laughing temptingly;
> my heart flutters in my breast,
> whenever I look quickly, for a moment—
> I say nothing, my tongue broken,
> a delicate fire runs under my skin,
> my eyes see nothing, my ears roar,
> cold sweat rushes down me,
> trembling seizes me,
> I turn the color grass,
> to myself I seem
> needing but little to die.
>
> But all must be endured, since . . .

This passage is *almost* purely expressive, "almost" in that the lines up to the semicolon largely set the scene: how else would we know what triggers the remaining, paradigmatically expressive lines? In the latter, Sappho's passion seems to be expressing itself; is so overwhelming it's as if it's blowing an exit hole through her chest. True, it's Sappho, not her passion, who speaks to a "you"—the woman she's on fire for—in the third line. But it's not as if Sappho actually expects to be heard by this temptress. One might say the poet is speaking to herself, but that doesn't seem quite right either; one doesn't sense the presence of an internal interlocutor as one does in a meditative poem or a soliloquy. The pressure behind Sappho's speaking is so strong that it obliterates any sense of a listening. Does this make the expressing in this poem, to invoke Wordsworth's term, an effusion? I'd call it more breathless than effusive—and even in its breathlessness, it manages a sort of clinical objectivity in anatomizing a passion into distinct facets of sensation.

A classical poem of expression that's less—much less—effusive still is the famous two-liner by Catullus known, per its opening words, as "Odi et Amo" (I hate and I love). The translations I've seen of this poem differ mainly in details. Here's the anonymous, straightforward one in Wikipedia:

> *Odi et amo. Quare id faciam fortasse requiris.*
> *Nescio, sed fieri sentio et excrucior.*

> I hate and I love. Why do I do this, perhaps you ask.
> I do not know, but I feel it happening and I am tortured.

This poem is an atom of expression, the minimal possible bit of it. Yet even an atom has its constituents. The nucleus of the poem is "I hate and I love . . . I am tortured," but this carries with it the electron cloud of "Why do I do this, perhaps you ask. / I do not know, but I feel it happening." As in Sappho's poem, a "you" is mentioned, but here it refers to us, the reader. And unlike Sappho's "you," this one is truly, if tangentially, addressed. I'm tempted to say that "Odi et Amo," for all its minuteness, both expresses and, in its touch of speech to a "you," addresses. If I file the poem as principally expressive, it's because the helpless bafflement

4

exposed by its addressing—"Why do I do this . . . I do not know"—is itself an emotion, one that supplements (and complicates) the expression of hate cum love to yield a work of feeling in every particle.

Unlike the previous two poems, a poem that unquestionably effuses is Gerard Manley Hopkins's sonnet "'Thou art indeed just, Lord, if I contend'" (1889). Hopkins takes his Latin epigraph from the biblical Book of Jeremiah. (It's translated in the poem's first three lines.)

*Justus quidem tu es, Domine, si disputem tecum; verumtamen
justa loquar ad te: Quare via impiorum prosperatur? &c.*

Thou art indeed just, Lord, if I contend
With thee; but, sir, so what I plead is just.
Why do sinners' ways prosper? and why must
Disappointment all I endeavour end?
  Wert thou my enemy, O thou my friend,
How wouldst thou worse, I wonder, than thou dost
Defeat, thwart me? Oh, the sots and thralls of lust
Do in spare hours more thrive than I that spend,
Sir, life upon thy cause. See, banks and brakes
Now, leavèd how thick! lacèd they are again
With fretty chervil, look, and fresh wind shakes
Them; birds build—but not I build; no, but strain,
Time's eunuch, and not breed one work that wakes.
Mine, O thou lord of life, send my roots rain.

A moment on the meter in this poem. Compared to the meter in Hopkins's famous nature sonnets of 1877 ("God's Grandeur," "Pied Beauty," best known of all, "The Windhover"), the meter here is fundamentally conventional. In the earlier poems, we find Hopkins at the height of his experimentation with what he called "sprung rhythm": meter released into unaccustomed freedom through an allowance of many unstressed syllables between stressed ones—this run of four of them, for example, in "The Windhover," in which Hopkins says that his heart

| | | |

Stirred for a bird,—the achieve of, the mastery of the thing!

There are no such runs in "'Thou art indeed just.'" Why? Several answers suggest themselves. To take the best one first, who knows? Perhaps, as can happen with any novelty, Hopkins was simply growing tired of sprung rhythm. Or perhaps he still quickened to its possibilities but, with the passage of the years, found himself feeling there was also a place in his work for meter of a more orthodox sort. Which suggests a related answer: that sprung rhythm seemed to him unsuitable, or at least suboptimal, for this particular poem. Sprung rhythm, after all, is among other things a kind of playing around, and the substance of "'Thou art indeed just'"—despair, even self-disgust—may have seemed too serious for play at even its highest minded.

I said that Catullus's "Odi et amo" addresses as well as expresses. So much the more so with "'Thou art indeed just.'" Hopkins couldn't be addressing someone, or Someone, more overtly. But expressing, not addressing, is what "'Thou are indeed just'" does most essentially. The poem is especially striking for the baldness and force of its expression. These qualities derive largely from rhetorical gestures: anguished, unanswerable questions ("Why do sinners' ways prosper? and why must / Disappointment all I endeavour end?"); hyperbole ("Wert thou my enemy, O thou my friend, / How wouldst thou worse, I wonder, than thou dost / Defeat, thwart me?"); a jamming together and tortuous ordering of words ("defeat, thwart"; "but not I build") that communicates an emotional extremity with no time or room for the niceties of syntax . . . all culminating in the thunderous *Mine,* whose power comes both from the word's being a standalone accent at the head of its line—the poem's only such—and from its getting ahead of what's being said: as though the poet's plea to "bring my life rain" is so urgent it can't wait for its full enunciation. When I say this poem effuses, it's in these rhetorical gestures as well as a number of eruptive interjections—"Oh," "See," "how thick!" "look," with "Mine" as the tremendous last—that it does so.

In the poems we've looked at so far, expressing shares the stage with another way of saying: with evoking in Sappho's scene setting or with addressing in "Odi et Amo" and, especially, "'Thou art indeed just.'" If expression pure and simple is what you're after, a good place to find it is in lyrics for music. I've mentioned the operatic aria as a prime site of such expression, but the same applies to words for music of any sort (unsurprisingly, since the singer of anything has ipso facto been moved beyond speech). Finding a purely expressive song lyric is like fishing an overstocked pond, but an example that jumped at my line before my hook even hit the water is Oscar Hammerstein's lyric for "(I'm in Love With) A Wonderful Guy," from the Rodgers and Hammerstein musical *South Pacific:*

I'm as corny as Kansas in August,
I'm as normal as blueberry pie.
No more a smart little girl with no heart,
I have found me a wonderful guy!

I am in a conventional dither,
With a conventional star in my eye.
And you will note there's a lump in my throat
When I speak of that wonderful guy!

I'm as trite and as gay as a daisy in May,
A cliché comin' true!
I'm bromidic and bright as a moon-happy night
Pourin' light on the dew!

I'm as corny as Kansas in August,
High as a flag on the Fourth of July!
If you'll excuse an expression I use,
I'm in love, I'm in love,
I'm in love, I'm in love,
I'm in love with a wonderful guy!

As light and content to charm as this lyric is, it's not without a *little* heft, in that the character who sings it, Nurse Nelly Forbush, is a bit of an intellectual. Or at least she's been one until now: "no more," she says, is she "a smart little girl with no heart," though her distance on corniness and normality, not to mention her acquaintance with *bromidic*, suggests an intelligence that will survive the bliss of infatuation.

But it's this bliss, of course, that every word of the song is fundamentally about. When Nelly says she's "high as a flag on the Fourth of July," she's saying pretty much everything she and the song have to say. But how deftly it's said! If I wanted to argue that Hammerstein is a giant of American poetry, this isn't the first lyric I'd adduce. (For that I'd go with "Ol' Man River.") But neither would I want to overlook a felicity like "conventional dither," a piece of compression Emily Dickinson wouldn't have been ashamed of. Nor would I want to undervalue the song's skein of similes, most of which are only being wittily appropriate in their *own* conventionalness, or its effortless-seeming internal rhymes, the elegant soft-shoe of "if you'll excuse an expression I use" being a particular triumph in this line. And all this mastery is capped by a risky recourse to five (!) straight "I'm in love's." This simplest of expedients captures the spinning of Nelly's head at least as well as any of the more complex artistry that precedes it. True, this gamble by Hammerstein receives vital support from Rodgers's dizzily repeating melody and ever-intensifying harmony. The payoff is one of the "American songbook's" most exhilarating endings.

Another example of purely expressive poetry isn't a song lyric, but that doesn't prevent it from being supremely lyrical. One of the better things about U.S. citizenship is the right to say that a countryman of yours wrote the following:

> The spotted hawk swoops by and accuses me, he complains of my gab
> and my loitering.
> I too am not a bit tamed, I too am untranslatable,
> I sound my barbaric yawp over the roofs of the world.
>
> The last scud of day holds back for me,
> It flings my likeness after the rest and true as any on the shadow'd wilds,
> It coaxes me to the vapor and the dusk.

I depart as air, I shake my white locks at the runaway sun,
I effuse my flesh in eddies, and drift it in lacy jags.

There's more verbal music in these free verse lines, which open the iconic
last section of Walt Whitman's *Song of Myself,* than in many rhymed and
metered stretches of comparable length. I'll spare you a blow by blow
of all the alliteration, assonance, and rhythmic repetition in this passage. But note, among its nonmusical strokes, the way a single word,
accuses, is all it takes to communicate the hawk's haughty wildness, the
magnificent indignation with which the hawk's indictment is resisted
(the author "too" is not "a bit tamed," is—another coup of diction—
"untranslatable"), the way the last line projects visuals for which the
obvious descriptor, *psychedelic,* didn't yet exist. . . . I'll leave perhaps the
best, certainly the best known, of these strokes to yawp for itself.

This passage is self-evidently expressive, but of what? Of an emotion, by the definition of expressiveness we're working with, but which
one? You could call it "elation," but only if you can live with doing
insufficient justice to its amplitude. Having offered these lines as a
case of pure expression, I should acknowledge that the immediately
succeeding ones, which conclude *Song of Myself,* effect one of the great
way-of-saying pivots—from expression to address—in poetry:

I bequeath myself to the dirt to grow from the grass I love,
If you want me again look for me under your boot soles.

You will hardly know who I am or what I mean,
But I shall be good health to you nevertheless,
And filter and fibre your blood.

Failing to fetch me at first keep encouraged,
Missing me one place search another,
I stop somewhere waiting for you.

The huge move here to explicit speech-to-the-reader owes much of
its masterful, magical ease to the transitional hinge—the first two of
these lines—on which it turns.

SOME POEMS THAT SAY BY EVOKING

A poem that says by evoking tries to make an object, a place, a person—a something—present to the reader. I might have called this way of saying "describing," rather than "evoking," but in using the latter term, I mean to suggest the possibility of a more ambitious and transporting operation. A poem that says purely by evoking is one we've touched on already, Tennyson's "The Eagle." It warrants a closer look.

> He clasps the crag with crooked hands;
> Close to the sun in lonely lands,
> Ring'd with the azure world he stands.
>
> The wrinkled sea beneath him crawls;
> He watches from his mountain walls,
> And like a thunderbolt he falls.

Shutter snapped, mission accomplished. No poem is less in need of explication, which leaves us unusually free to appreciate its felicities. It's shot through, for instance, with the word music for which Tennyson is famous. Its first line alone sports no fewer than three instances of alliteration and three more of assonance. Every line in the poem features at least one of these devices (even the last, which may seem an exception but in which the vowel-plus-*l* kinship of -*bolt* and *falls* does some unobtrusive binding). The poem is also replete with swerves from the expectable. To call an eagle's talons "crooked" is intriguingly odd; to call them "hands" is marvelously odder still. Even allowing for the precedent of Icarus, "close to the sun" isn't how just any poet would convey the height of a cliff, any more than your average poet would see the world, a century before the invention of the fish-eye lens, as "ringing" the eagle. If "wrinkled" sea is the poem's most striking coup of diction, its subtlest may be the way the eagle "watches" (intransitive), suggesting the raptor's stillness in scanning a vast surround for the slightest sign of prey. *Thunderbolt* may be a little sensationalistic, but that's not to gainsay its effectiveness: it stands out (like a jagged bolt of lightning?) in being the poem's only word of more than two syllables. You'd think *thunderbolt*'s length might impede the poem's movement, but the second of its two metrical stresses (*-bolt*) is so light in comparison with its first (*thun-*) that the word positively races across the metrical grid, suggesting the velocity of the eagle's plummet.

Beyond these particular strokes, the poem is admirable for the patterning of its overall structure. Each of its stanzas is identically divided into two parts: a one-line declarative sentence (don't be fooled by its ending with a semicolon), followed by a two-line sentence whose inverted syntax puts an active verb phrase—*he stands* and the cognate, poem-clinching *he falls*—at its conclusion. The congruence of these stanzas is directly perceptible to the ear, a kind of rhyme writ large.

A poem that's largely but not purely evocative is Wordsworth's sonnet "Composed upon Westminster Bridge, September 3, 1802."

Earth has not anything to show more fair:
Dull would he be of soul who could pass by
A sight so touching in its majesty:
This City now doth, like a garment, wear
The beauty of the morning; silent, bare,
Ships, towers, domes, theatres, and temples lie
Open unto the fields, and to the sky;
All bright and glittering in the smokeless air.
Never did sun more beautifully steep
In his first splendour, valley, rock, or hill;
Ne'er saw I, never felt, a calm so deep!
The river glideth at his own sweet will:
Dear God! the very houses seem asleep;
And all that mighty heart is lying still!

This poem goes about its evoking in a more complicated way than "The Eagle" (and in doing so throws into relief the latter's strict adherence to description). Two aspects of complication are involved. One is a kind of special pleading on the depicted scene's behalf. No sight could be more fair; only someone dull of soul could fail to be moved by its majesty; never did sun fall more beautifully on a vista—not much room for disagreement with these hyperbolic claims. (When Keats said we resent poetry that "has a palpable design upon us," he might have put these assertions into evidence.) Whereas "Ne'er saw I, never felt a calm so deep" is different: less an insisting on the scene's calmness than an averral of feeling in the face of it. Wordsworth offers a touch of expression, that is to say, in a poem whose principal business is evocation. The evoking here is also complicated by something only a grump would object to: the poem's figural touches. These are mainly of personification: the city "like a garment, wears" the morning's beauty; the sun steeps the landscape in "his" splendor; the river glides at "his" will; the houses seem "asleep," and of course—one of the unforgettable figures in poetry—the "mighty heart" that all of London, taken together and viewed entire, is. This figuration and, yes, the poet's special pleading combine to project a kind of aureole around the poem's descriptive core.

"The Eagle" evokes a creature. "Composed upon Westminster Bridge" evokes a scene. "Miniver Cheevy," an anthology piece by Edward Arlington Robinson, evokes . . . guess what (and whom)?

Miniver Cheevy, child of scorn,
   Grew lean while he assailed the seasons;
He wept that he was ever born,
   And he had reasons.

Miniver loved the days of old
   When swords were bright and steeds were prancing;
The vision of a warrior bold
   Would set him dancing.

Miniver sighed for what was not,
   And dreamed, and rested from his labors;
He dreamed of Thebes and Camelot,
   And Priam's neighbors.

Miniver mourned the ripe renown
   That made so many a name so fragrant;

He mourned Romance, now on the town,
  And Art, a vagrant.

Miniver loved the Medici,
  Albeit he had never seen one;
He would have sinned incessantly
  Could he have been one.

Miniver cursed the commonplace
  And eyed a khaki suit with loathing;
He missed the mediæval grace
  Of iron clothing.

Miniver scorned the gold he sought,
  But sore annoyed was he without it;
Miniver thought, and thought, and thought,
  And thought about it.

Miniver Cheevy, born too late,
  Scratched his head and kept on thinking;
Miniver coughed, and called it fate,
  And kept on drinking.

Not the most nuanced of portraits—in fact, a bit of a cartoon—but it's hard to hold this against so enjoyable a performance. Miniver is largely defined by a single attribute the poem wastes no time in revealing: a love of "the days of old." That said, the very first thing we hear about Miniver is that he's a "child of scorn." The rhetorical ring of this phrase—common in Robinson's work and not always to its benefit—may cause us to give the phrase less consideration than it deserves. Isn't Robinson intimating that Miniver's parents were what we now call emotionally abusive? If so, mightn't such mistreatment help explain the flight of Miniver's maturing imagination into the refuge of an idealized historical past? Whatever one makes of *child of scorn*, it's as much as Robinson has to say about Miniver's beginnings. Whether he should have said at least a little more, or whether saying even a little more would have overloaded the poem (and/or undermined its essential if rueful buoyancy), is the sort of question writers are perpetually bedeviled by.

The poem as a whole offers a series of mainly humorous riffs on Miniver's love of an Arthurian past. Lest we be tempted to relegate the poem to the realm of light verse, we shouldn't lose sight of wit's central- ity to poetry, serious and humorous alike. I'm reminded of something Robert Frost said about the fourth "thought" in the poem's penulti- mate stanza: not that it's funny (which it is) but that it exemplifies "the intolerable touch of poetry" (a reference to Shelley's "Ozymandias," with its "intolerable touch of time"). Speaking of Frost-Robinson relations, we find in "Miniver Cheevy" bits of the sort of colloquial speech—"he had reasons," "on the town," "kept on thinking and drinking"—that Frost credited *himself* with bringing to verse. (Frost's admiration for Robinson, while never hidden outright, was always kept under a bit of a bushel—perhaps, one feels, because Frost owed more to Robinson than he was comfortable letting on.) Yet Robinson is also able to find a nondisruptive home in "Miniver" for a few archaic locutions ("war- rior bold," "sore annoyed," "days of old" itself), as befits a poem largely concerned with its protagonist's fixation on the distant past.

Another much-anthologized poem, by Robert Hayden, evokes two people and the relationship between them.

THOSE WINTER SUNDAYS

Sundays too my father got up early
and put his clothes on in the blueblack cold,
then with cracked hands that ached
from labor in the weekday weather made
banked fires blaze. No one ever thanked him.

I'd wake and hear the cold splintering, breaking.
When the rooms were warm, he'd call,
and slowly I would rise and dress,
fearing the chronic angers of that house,

Speaking indifferently to him,
who had driven out the cold
and polished my good shoes as well.
What did I know, what did I know
of love's austere and lonely offices?

This deeply moving poem resides in my memory as a sonnet per usual, in rhyming pentameter. I can see why I misremember it this way. It does have fourteen lines (though their 5-4-5 disposition is unusual), but my sense of it as a sonnet, which it's clearly meant to be, owes as much or more to its lapidary language, especially that of its last line, whose unforgettable *offices* has a resonant and arresting elevation. It always comes as a little shock to see, when I revisit this poem, that it doesn't contain any rhymes, at least no perfect ones. (There's a rhyme-ish relation between *ached* and *made*, and an off-rhyme between *dress* and *house*.) And only half of the poem's lines are in pentameter, though all of them are scannable in standard feet, and the wonderful last line is a pentameter par excellence.

The poem is studded with coups of diction that begin as soon as its second word, a *too* that tells us the father labored every day, Sundays included. *Blueback* is a striking, synesthetic adjective for "cold": there's no suggestion of any *thing* being blue and/or black; blueness and blackness are presented, rather, as attributes of coldness itself. (Hayden evokes the cold even more strikingly, and again synesthetically, in hearing it "splintering, breaking." What's literally heard, one presumes, is the breaking of sticklike pieces of frigid wood—logs being unavailable or perhaps unaffordable—for the banked fires the father is building.) In addition to its brilliance as diction, *blueblack* is part of a masterful sound complex (*blueback, cracked, ached*). In fact the whole first stanza compares with anything by Tennyson in musicality, with its healthy helpings of assonance (*father/got, labor/made*), internal off-rhyme (*got/put*), alliteration (*banked/blaze*)—even an internal perfect rhyme (*banked/thanked*).

The relationship between Hayden and his father, evoked in just a couple of strokes, is complicated. *Chronic angers* indicts the father straightforwardly enough, but the son's "indifference" suggests an explanation, even justification, for these angers. (Here's a poem that really is "confessional" in admitting a poet's condemnation, for a change, of himself.) There can't be many poems born in the heart that gain more from a passage through so subtle an intelligence.

An ancient species of poetry evokes a visual artwork. The oldest Western example of such "ekphrastic" poetry is the famous description in the *Iliad* of the heavily (to put it mildly) decorated shield that Vulcan forges for Achilles. (An early-model drone, in the person of the sea nymph Thetis, is standing by to air-deliver the finished product.) Here, to give you a sense of the passage, are its beginning and end—a very small portion—in Alexander Pope's translation:

> Then first he form'd the immense and solid shield;
> Rich various artifice emblazed the field;
> Its utmost verge a threefold circle bound;
> A silver chain suspends the massy round;
> Five ample plates the broad expanse compose,
> And godlike labours on the surface rose.
> There shone the image of the master-mind:
> There earth, there heaven, there ocean he design'd;
> The unwearied sun, the moon completely round;
> The starry lights that heaven's high convex crown'd;
> The Pleiads, Hyads, with the northern team;
> And great Orion's more refulgent beam;
> To which, around the axle of the sky,
> The Bear, revolving, points his golden eye,
> Still shines exalted on the ethereal plain,
> Nor bathes his blazing forehead in the main.
> . . . .
> Thus the broad shield complete the artist crown'd
> With his last hand, and pour'd the ocean round:
> In living silver seem'd the waves to roll,
> And beat the buckler's verge, and bound the whole.

This done, whate'er a warrior's use requires
He forged; the cuirass that outshone the fires,
The greaves of ductile tin, the helm impress'd
With various sculpture, and the golden crest.
At Thetis' feet the finished labour lay:
She, as a falcon cuts the aerial way,
Swift from Olympus' snowy summit flies,
And bears the blazing present through the skies.

This founding example of ekphrasis is typical of many that followed in never deviating from its mission of description. It's as though the challenge and promise of bringing the visual to a new life in language is huge enough to occupy the poet totally: if one can do this, the thinking seems to be, one has done enough. (I'm reminded of the pursuit of pure depiction in those still-life paintings that overflow with crystal and muslin and other such luxuries.) In focusing exclusively on the "what" at the possible expense of the "what about," a strict ekphrasis runs the risk of absorbing the writer more than the reader. If Homer's shield passage holds our interest over its hundreds of lines—and I'm not saying this *isn't* an if—its doing so is a tour de force (with no small tip of the hat to Pope's virtuosically versified translation). However impressively Homer and Pope rise to their formidable challenge, the sense of release as Thetis launches off from Olympus, shield in hand— or, if she knows what's good for her, with her arms wrapped tightly around it—is at least partly owing to the passage's being sprung, at its conclusion, from its lengthy commitment to inventory. (This isn't to discount the thrill of its last-minute shift to the present tense.)

Pure ekphrases, like the shield description, shouldn't blind us to the existence of ekphrases whose motives are mixed—even, sometimes, extremely mixed. To say that Keats's "Ode on a Grecian Urn" describes an artwork is like saying that the Gettysburg Address commemorates a battle—true as far it goes. The urn is less an occasion for description than a springboard for flights of imagination: I'm thinking in particular of the "little town" that sits "emptied" of the people enacting the sylvan rites on the vessel. (And this isn't even to mention Keats's vision of a future in which the urn will give unborn generations its famous two cents on the relation between truth and beauty.) To take another such case, it's true that Rainer Maria Rilke's best-known poem describes an "Archaic Torso of Apollo" but only in the course of suggesting an artistic beauty so overwhelming as to require you to "change your life."

To go by its title (the name of a village in Gloucestershire), Edward Thomas's most popular poem might be expected to evoke a place.

ADLESTROP

Yes. I remember Adlestrop—
The name, because one afternoon
Of heat the express-train drew up there
Unwontedly. It was late June.

The steam hissed. Someone cleared his throat.
No one left and no one came
On the bare platform. What I saw
Was Adlestrop—only the name

And willows, willow-herb, and grass,
And meadowsweet, and haycocks dry,
No whit less still and lonely fair
Than the high cloudlets in the sky.

And for that minute a blackbird sang
Close by, and round him, mistier,
Farther and farther, all the birds
Of Oxfordshire and Gloucestershire.

Is it a place, precisely, that this poem evokes? I ask because, judging by Thomas's account of his stop at Adlestrop, there was, as Gertrude Stein said of her native Oakland, no there there: just a station sign and a natural surround whose elements Thomas selectively (if, we sense, lovingly) details. In saying at the poem's outset that all he remembers of Adlestrop is "the name," Thomas is already intimating that, for purposes of this poem, *Adlestrop* will denominate not a place so much as something less tangible.

That something might be called a moment. The poem can in fact be viewed as evoking two moments: the "still" one that attends the stopped train, and a conversation from some time after. The latter is implied by the striking "Yes." that jump-starts the poem. It's as though Thomas has just been asked if he knows a place called Adlestrop. "Yes." (full stop, as though he's taking a moment to confirm the realization to himself): "I remember Adlestrop." It's a little surprising to learn that this "Yes." (though with no period after it) was already in the first of the poem's several drafts. Maybe the word was tossed in initially to fill out the meter, but one imagines Thomas instantly quickening to the conversational, even dramatic charge it gives the poem's opening. (The period after the *Yes* doesn't appear until Thomas's third draft, having been preceded in the second by a comma. To attribute this revision string to "craft" would be to underappreciate its minute adjustments toward aural fidelity, adjustments that reflect an exquisite sensitivity to the rhythms of speech.)

Of course, the moment "Adlestrop" mainly evokes is that of the stopped train. Journalist that he sometimes was, Thomas wastes no time in providing the who, what, when, and where of this (non)event. As to its why, it would seem that there wasn't any, at least no apparent one. All Thomas has to say on this score is that the train, an express that would normally have gone tearing through this nowheresville, has pulled up there "unwontedly." Like the most accomplished sort of draftsman, Thomas evokes the train's minute-long stay at the platform with the merest handful of strokes. The first couple—the steam's hiss and the clearing of a throat—are auditory: aptly so, given how little there is to see, at least of the man-made variety. But sound is soon supplanted by sight, as Thomas's awareness expands to take in its natural element of nature. It moves from some items of greenery (specified with a precision peculiar to naturalists and Englishmen) to the wonderfully observed and wonderfully coined "cloudlets" in the sky, an elevation of gaze both literal and symbolic. Note the deftness with which Thomas communicates the "still"-ness and "fair"-ness of all this: not by declaring these qualities but by subsuming them within a comparison, the greenery being "not a whit less" still or fair than the cloudlets above. Thomas's attention, while staying with the natural, now circles back to the auditory: at first to the singing of a single bird, then to the singing of many. It isn't that more birds have joined in; Thomas's awareness has expanded, rather, to take in farther, fainter, songs. In evoking them, Thomas achieves the poem's most inspired writing: first in lighting on the genius stroke of *mistier* to describe the sound of the distant birds, then in a close that weds a brilliant yet delicate rhyme (*mistier/Gloucestershire*) to a beautiful dying fall.

At its outset, one of William Butler Yeats's best-known poems reads like an ekphrasis. But what he's out to evoke isn't an artwork.

LEDA AND THE SWAN

A sudden blow: the great wings beating still
Above the staggering girl, her thighs caressed
By the dark webs, her nape caught in his bill,
He holds her helpless breast upon his breast.

How can those terrified vague fingers push
The feathered glory from her loosening thighs?
And how can body, laid in that white rush,
But feel the strange heart beating where it lies?

A shudder in the loins engenders there
The broken wall, the burning roof and tower
And Agamemnon dead.
                                    Being so caught up,
So mastered by the brute blood of the air,
Did she put on his knowledge with his power
Before the indifferent beak could let her drop?

There's no shortage of pictures depicting Leda's rape by Zeus-as-swan, but Yeats isn't evoking any of them here. The image he's working from hangs, rather, in the teeming gallery of his imagination. And what he's out to portray is less an image per se than, as with the last poem we looked at, a moment, one of the most terrible in classical mythology.

There are those who have a low opinion of adjectives in poetry. (Mary Oliver: "Every adjective and adverb is worth five cents. Every verb is worth fifty cents.") What, one wonders, are these admonitors to make of the veritable feast of adjectives that is "Leda and the Swan"? Yeats doesn't hesitate to modify one of the nouns here, *fingers,* with two adjectives, perhaps because both *terrified* and *vague* refer in a wonderfully estranging way not to Leda's fingers but to her whole self. This unusual device might be called "assisted synecdoche," in that we wouldn't see *fingers* as standing for the whole Leda without the help of its adjectives. Yeats finds the device so compelling that he brings it back for an encore with *indifferent beak.*

The poem has no shortage of unforgettable strokes ("body laid in that white rush"; the simple yet astonishing "strange heart" . . .), but my favorite may be a coup of syntax. Note that the second stanza is formed from a pair of rhetorical questions (the poem ends with yet a third; throughout his work, Yeats can't get enough of them). I use the term *formed* advisedly because these questions are conjoined in a near-symmetrical relationship, the *near-* being the best thing about the symmetry: "How can A 'push' B?" is mirrored, with an inverse twist, by "How can C 'but feel' D?" As an elegantly ingenious way of saying what Yeats, in the guise of asking, is saying, I don't see how this cross-stitching could be surpassed.

The moment evoked in "Leda" take place in its author's head. The same is true of the moment evoked in Keats's first great poem.

ON FIRST LOOKING INTO CHAPMAN'S HOMER

Much have I travell'd in the realms of gold,
And many goodly states and kingdoms seen;

Round many western islands have I been
Which bards in fealty to Apollo hold.
Oft of one wide expanse had I been told
That deep-brow'd Homer ruled as his demesne;
Yet did I never breathe its pure serene
Till I heard Chapman speak out loud and bold:
Then felt I like some watcher of the skies
When a new planet swims into his ken;
Or like stout Cortez when with eagle eyes
He star'd at the Pacific—and all his men
Look'd at each other with a wild surmise—
Silent, upon a peak in Darien.

It's true that what Keats portrays here, his first encounter with George Chapman's vigorous translation of Homer, took longer than a literal moment. The poem was sparked by an all-night session Keats and his friend Charles Clarke put in at Clarke's house, delightedly dipping into Clarke's rare copy of the Chapman volume. But as evoked in the poem (which, delivered either by a messenger or by Keats himself, was sitting on Clarke's breakfast table by ten the next morning!), Keats's realization via Chapman of Homer's vastness has the feel of an epiphanic instant.

Note the patience with which Keats sets this instant up: by telling us that coming into his evening at Clarke's he was already well versed in classical history and mythology; that he'd heard tell of how hugely Homer loomed in the classical realm (his saying he'd been "told of" Homer's work is a bit of poetic license—he'd read at least *The Iliad* already, if in a translation by Alexander Pope that he felt was mere versification); and that only when he looked into *Chapman's* translation did he first appreciate the true scope of the Homeric "expanse."

Keats doesn't hear Chapman "speak out loud and bold" until the eighth of this sonnet's fourteen lines. Having devoted all of its octave to setting this epiphany up, Keats has only its sestet in which to evoke it. Many poets would be happy to call it a career were they to come up with either of the wondrous figures Keats now enlists in the evoking.

Ransacking his reading—news of the recent discovery of Uranus; an account, in William Robertson's *History of America,* of Balboa's discovery of the Pacific (not, notoriously, "Cortez's"; when Clarke immediately told Keats of his mistake, Keats shrugged a giant's shrug)—Keats lands one of the great one-two image punches in poetry. Reeling as we are from the first of these haymakers, the watcher's sighting of a new planet, we're in no condition to defend ourselves from its even more powerful sequel, a blow that, in the best tradition of the uppercut, knocks us out even as it lifts us off our feet.

I'd always thought the central magic in Keats's depiction of Cortez's (Balboa's) discovery—those speculative glances the men exchange with one another—was a product of pure imagining. So I was surprised to learn recently that, according to Robertson's account of the discovery, something of the sort actually occurred. Here's the passage in question:

> At length the Indians assured them, that from the top of the next mountain they should discover the ocean which was the object of their wishes. When, with infinite toil, they had climbed up the greater part of the steep ascent, Balboa commanded his men to halt, and advanced alone to the summit, that he might be the first who should enjoy a spectacle which he had so long desired. As soon as he beheld the South Sea stretching in endless prospect below him, he fell on his knees, and lifting up his hands to Heaven, returned thanks to God. . . . His followers, observing his transports of joy, rushed forward to join in his wonder, exultation, and gratitude.

It's true that the "rushing forward" in this account is far less suggestive and dramatic than the exchange of glances Keats transmutes it to. And only a poet of genius would have couched the men's speculation as a "wild [!] surmise." Keats's gift also informs the attribution of *stout*—in, potentially, a couple of senses—to Cortez, as well as the coinage of "deep-browed Homer," itself a Homeric epithet. These adjective-noun conjunctions reflect Keats's famous desire to "load every rift with ore" (even as they pose, like "Leda," a serious problem for the contingent that frowns on adjectives in poetry). Of course, not every stroke of diction in this poem involves an adjective: the new planet, for instance, "swims" into its discoverer's "ken." And not least of the poem's triumphs is its entire last line, which offers, within a commanding overall rhythm, the arresting, initial *Silent,* the alliteration of *peak* with *upon,* and the breathtaking close on the surprise-rhyming *Darien.* To appreciate such particulars is to be reminded that even the most inspired poetic idea is fully realized only in words that are worthy of it (which isn't to say, the opinion of some notable poets notwithstanding, that there's no such thing as an inspired poetic idea). Keats was twenty-one when he wrote this poem. If, as some evidence suggests, he already "surmised" his poetic capacities when he sat down to write it, he must have been sure of them by the time he finished it.

The poems we've considered so far in this section have evoked, successively, a creature, a scene, a person, two people (and the relationship between them), an artwork, and, in a movement toward the less tangible, what I've called moments: of peace at a village train station, of mythical violence, of epiphany in a great mind's development. A poem by George Herbert evokes something less tangible still: a concept. Here's the first of two poems entitled "Prayer" in his collection *The Temple:*

PRAYER (1)

Prayer the church's banquet, angel's age,
    God's breath in man returning to his birth,
    The soul in paraphrase, heart in pilgrimage,
    The Christian plummet sounding heav'n and earth
Engine against th' Almighty, sinner's tow'r,
    Reversed thunder, Christ-side-piercing spear,
    The six-days world transposing in an hour,
    A kind of tune, which all things hear and fear;
Softness, and peace, and joy, and love, and bliss,
    Exalted manna, gladness of the best,
    Heaven in ordinary, man well drest,

The milky way, the bird of Paradise,
Church-bells beyond the stars heard, the soul's blood,
The land of spices; something understood.

Thinking the better of trying to define prayer directly, Herbert approaches the subject of this extraordinary sonnet from myriad angles of figuration and comparison. But this account of his method doesn't accord, or accords only incompletely, with one's experience of the poem. For even as each of his equivalents for prayer contributes to a "composite" picture of it, each of them also comes across as a free-standing representation of it. One might say that prayer is defined here not only as "this plus this plus this . . ." but also as "this and this and this . . . ." On the latter understanding, prayer seems a concept that can spawn no end of definitions, all equally adequate to their source, rather as all points in the universe have equal claim to being at its center, their having all been one at its beginning.

Despite the seeming modernity of "Prayer (I)" as a pure "string" of definitions with no syntactical connection from one to the next, none of these definitions is difficult in the modern sense. Some of them— for example, "softness, and peace, and joy, and love, and bliss," "gladness of the best"—are almost ostentatiously simple, as though to say, "Why even try to wax poetic about something so fundamental?" Another poet might have saved the poem's most striking representation of prayer, the breathtaking "Church-bells beyond the stars heard," for last, but Herbert, being Herbert, ends with the plainest of them: "something understood." In being preceded by a semicolon, these closing words comes across as both final and summary, a deep-focus duality that might give pause, or more, to those who frown upon the semicolon in verse. "Something understood" can be read as something understood by an all-understanding God and/or as something whose nature *we* understand, and understand (per *understood* in the sense of *assumed*) implicitly. Viewed from the latter perspective, "Prayer (I)" provides a mind-stretching series of definitions of its subject, only to end with a definition that implies we had an intrinsic knowledge of prayer all along. This ending resonates like little else in letters. How it does this will never be wholly knowable, though only a tin-eared critic would think the effect has nothing to do with word music: with the assonance of *some-* and *under-;* with the off-rhyme of *-stood* and *blood*—not least of all, with the consecutive trochees in **SOMEthing UNderstood,** which help drive the poem's last line, and the poem as a whole, so ineluctably home.

Sometimes a poet will try to evoke something so intangible as to seemingly defy evocation. If there was ever a poet equipped to take on this challenge, it was Emily Dickinson. In the following poem, #673 in Thomas Johnson's edition, we see her deploying this equipment to astonishing effect.

> The Love a Life can show Below
> Is but a filament, I know,
> Of that diviner thing
> That faints upon the face of Noon—
> And smites the Tinder in the Sun—
> And hinders Gabriel's Wing—
>
> 'Tis this—in Music—hints and sways—
> And far abroad on Summer days—
> Distils uncertain pain—
> 'Tis this enamors in the East—
> And tints the Transit in the West
> With harrowing Iodine—
>
> 'Tis this—invites—appalls—endows—
> Flits—glimmers—proves—dissolves—
> Returns—suggests—convicts—enchants—
> Then—flings in Paradise—

What is this "thing" that's diviner than any earthly love? Dickinson knows better than to try to say. If she nonetheless seems to say, it's because she's so profusely brilliant in telling us what the thing in question does.

Anyone who's attended even a few poetry workshops may well have heard a poem praised for the energy supplied by its verbs. I can imagine the reclusive Dickinson sitting at a workshop table, if one emplaced in her bedroom. Glancing shyly about at her fellow participants (God knows what manner of being is facilitating), she softly ventures: "If verbs are desired . . ." and passes around copies of a poem with the cryptic title of "673." The silence that greets the bevy of verbs in the poem reflects bafflement and/or a sense that, as Randall Jarrell wrote of some lines by Whitman, mere praise would be tantamount to insolence.

The verbs in the poem at first behave normally from a grammatical standpoint. The transitive ones have direct objects (*smites* → *Tinder*, *hinders* → *Wing*, *distils* → *pain*, *tints* → *Transit*). The first few intransitive verbs have either an indirect object ("faints upon the Face of Noon") or no object ("hints and sways"). So far so usual, until we hit, and are hit by, "enamors in the East." *Enamor* is an oddity among verbs. It's classed as transitive—that is, it takes a direct object—but usually does so passively, as in *enamored of* or *enamored with*. Less commonly, it can also take its direct object actively, as in "she enamored him," meaning she charmed him (or more). What you never encounter, unless you're wandering in the wilds of #673, is *enamor* without an object at all. I'll let a licensed grammarian tell you exactly how *enamors* functions in "enamors in the East," but I will say that the word takes on, in this unique usage, an unaccustomed autonomy.

Now comes a move that lifts the poem into an unaccustomed speech realm altogether: Dickinson's casting of its last stanza in, essentially, nothing *but* verbs. She deals these seriatim, with only the most attenuated hint of syntax. They strike, rather, in a rapid succession that jostles one's thinking progressively freer. (This succession may call to mind Herbert's syntaxless string of definitions in "Prayer [I]," which spins us similarly beyond sequential logic into a more syncretic mode of understanding.) In resorting to this extraordinary principle of construction, Dickinson is telling us between the lines—or in this case, the words—how difficult it is to evoke her "diviner thing" *in* words. Note that every verb in this stanza lacks—or, perhaps better in this context, is unencumbered by—an object, direct or indirect. This objectlessness is, for the intransitive verbs among them—*flits, glimmers, dissolves* (this one can be transitive but isn't here), *returns* (which can also be transitive if you're at a customer service desk or on a tennis court)—business as usual. But what about the stanza's transitive verbs, that is, most of its others, climaxing in the exhilarating *flings?* In lacking an object, these take on an autonomy foreshadowed by that of the preceding, freestanding *enamors*—and become, like the freestanding *enamors,* somewhat estranged in the process from their normal usage. (I'm reminded of T. S. Eliot's observation that words in poetry are sometimes "dislocated" into an alteration of meaning.) In making the verbs in this stanza objectless as well as all but syntaxless, Dickinson redoubles the daring of her attempt to evoke something seemingly unevocable.

SOME POEMS THAT SAY BY ADDRESSING

A poem that says by addressing gives the impression of being spoken to a listener (or listeners, like those friends, Romans, and countrymen). If you stop to think about all the kinds of poems that answer to this description—verse letters, dramatic monologues, verse plays (whose characters speak to one another), eclogues in dialogue form, narratives (which are implicitly addressed to a circle of listeners sitting around a Platonic campfire), prayers, apostrophes, many odes (all of Keats's, for instance), declarations of love, not to forget meditations, which are often addressed to that listener called oneself—it's clear that more (probably much more) poetry mainly addresses than mainly expresses or evokes. (This only stands to reason, actual speech being language's natural habitat—notwithstanding Jacques Derrida's awarding of this distinction not to speech but to writing, as though to say, "Why merely be wrong when you can get something exactly backward?")

Some poems of address declare themselves as such explicitly, through their title, their genre, or their overt reference to a listener. Others do so implicitly, through a simulation of the tics and tells of spoken language. A familiar bit of such simulation is found in Robert Browning's dramatic monologue "My Last Duchess," when the Duke says of his latest, and late, Duchess, "She had / A heart—how shall I say—too soon made glad." That "how shall I say" captures the Duke

as a literal speaker, finding words at once eloquent and adroitly de-
fanged for what he sees as the Duchess's overgenerosity of affection.
An even better-known example of speech indicating an unfolding of
thought would be "To die, to sleep— / To sleep—perchance to dream:
ay, there's the rub." Such examples of simulated speech in poetry could
be endlessly multiplied. (There's a sense, of course, in which all poems
implicitly speak to someone—the reader—but in this section, I'll focus
on poems that posit an addressee more overtly.)

Consider, as a portal to the poetry of address, the little specimen
that prefaces the edition of Robert Frost's collected poems.

THE PASTURE

I'm going out to clean the pasture spring;
I'll only stop to rake the leaves away
(And wait to watch the water clear, I may):
I sha'n't be gone long.—You come too.

I'm going out to fetch the little calf
That's standing by the mother. It's so young,
It totters when she licks it with her tongue.
I sha'n't be gone long.—You come too.

Its title notwithstanding, how much does this poem really have to say
about a pasture? The question might be sharpened by putting it this
way: is "The Pasture" about a pasture the way Tennyson's "The Eagle"
is about an eagle? A defensible response would be "Not really."

Of course, the poem has *something* to do with a pasture. Maybe it's
less about a pasture per se than a visit to one. This, after all, is what the
whole first stanza is focused on: the speaker's purpose in going there
("to clean the pasture spring"), what this cleaning will entail ("raking
the leaves away"), a related thing the speaker may do ("wait to watch
the water clear"), and an invitation to "you" to come along. In the second stanza, the speaker offers another reason for the visit: to fetch a
calf that's standing by "the mother." (Ah, the power, in language, of
the smallest things: "its mother" would have made *mother* both less

iconic—less elevated from a particular mother to a representative of the maternal role in general—and less faithful to a country speaker's way of indicating that, where a very young calf is concerned, a mother's proximity is a given.) Frost supplies an ancillary if unforgettable detail about the calf ("It's so young, / It totters when she licks it with her tongue") but then resumes his proposal of a visit by repeating his invitation to come along.

So "The Pasture" may be more about a visit to a pasture than a pasture itself. But it may be most essentially about a third thing. Consider the invitation that ends each of the poem's stanzas. The invitee is "you." It's tempting, and partly correct, to take this "you" as us, the reader: the same "you" that Whitman "stops somewhere waiting for" at the end of *Song of Myself.* But Whitman is addressing a generalized "you" in no particular place, whereas "The Pasture" is set in, or on, a clearly particular place: the speaker's farm. As we read the poem, we see two people—speaker/inviter and listener/invitee—standing together in that setting. The listener, then, isn't, or isn't only, "you," the reader; he or she is also, and maybe principally, "you," an acquaintance of the speaker and, as such, a character in this poem. The poem's placing of speaker and listener in spatial and interpersonal relation qualifies it as, in however understated a way, a dramatic poem. (Frost: "Everything written is as good as it's dramatic.") To say this another way: in addition to whatever else it's about, "The Pasture" is about an interaction between people.

"You come too," says the speaker. But why would the listener *want* to come? To watch the speaker rake some leaves out of a spring? (I can hear a now-forgotten comedian named Jackie Vernon saying that the chief entertainment in his hometown of Pittsburgh was "watching ice drip off the back of a truck.") The speaker also says he may "wait to watch the water clear," a prospect that seems, if possible, less exciting still. But "clarity" is a suggestive concept in Frost. In "The Figure a Poem Makes," he famously says that a poem ideally "begins in delight . . . runs a course of lucky events, and ends in a clarification of life—not necessarily a great clarification, such as sects and cults are founded on, but in a momentary stay against confusion." In his poem "For Once,

Then, Something," Frost tells of looking down into a well at its reflection of a "summer heaven" (starring, he half-humorously admits, his own gazing face) and discerning

> as I thought, beyond the picture,
> Through the picture, a something white, uncertain,
> Something more of the depths—and then I lost it.
> Water came to rebuke the too clear water.
> One drop fell from a fern, and lo, a ripple
> Shook whatever it was lay there at bottom,
> Blurred it, blotted it out. What was that whiteness?
> Truth? A pebble of quartz? For once, then, something.

"*Too* clear water"? As in clearer than we deserve? Clearer than any self-respecting universe would grant the likes of *us?* When Frost says in "The Pasture" that he may "wait to watch the water clear," it's no great stretch to think he'd be watching for a physical indication of something metaphysical. Given the placement of "The Pasture" as preface to Frost's collected poems, the poet may be quietly alerting us here to a metaphysical element in the book as a whole.

Nor is that all "The Pasture" augurs with regard to the *Collected*. Consider the second task the poem evokes, the fetching of the calf. Frost's account of it previews some additional aspects of his work. There's the sharp observing of a rural milieu: Frost may not be the first writer to notice that a very young calf "totters" when its mother licks it, but he may well be the first to find the phenomenon worth mentioning. There's also the way he mentions it: the actual qualities, and quality, of the writing. Beyond the vividness of *totters* itself, the word's alliteration with *tongue* adds music to the line that contains it. (A possible strike against this line is the redundancy of licking something "with a tongue," though this apparent gaffe may be part of what makes the mother's licking so visualizable.) Note as well the way the mother-calf interaction infuses feeling into the poem, an indication that Frost's work will have room in it for metaphysics and sentiment alike. A species of feeling is in fact at the heart of "The Pasture." Call

SUBJECT AS SOMETHING TO SAY

it fellow feeling, between an inviter and invitee who also represent
writer and reader. "I'm about to embark, in the book you're holding,
on an adventure in thinking, feeling, making, living," says Frost. "You
come too."

"The Pasture" is a poem of address mainly by virtue of its "you." So
is one of W. C. Williams's best-known poems. Like "The Pasture," it
contains an imperative that's not a command, though where Frost's
"You come too" was more an encouragement, Williams's "Forgive me"
is more a plea (if one that grins a little).

THIS IS JUST TO SAY

I have eaten
the plums
that were in
the icebox

and which
you were probably
saving
for breakfast

Forgive me
they were delicious
so sweet
and so cold.

This is presumably addressed to Williams's wife; it's hard not to imagine it as a note stuck on the refrigerator door, which would make
it maybe the shortest verse letter ever. What is *this* poem's subject?
Certainly, in part, the theft of those sweet, cold plums. But like "The
Pasture," the poem is most essentially about people. What sort of person eats the plums his wife was "probably" saving for breakfast? The
sort who can't stop himself from doing so, of course, but also the sort
who sees his doing so as an affirmation, to himself and his wife alike,
of sensuous, even sensual, "deliciousness." One feels, on this reading,

that Williams's wife will forgive him and that he knows she will. Does Williams address only his wife in this poem? He may not be speaking to us explicitly, but he knows we're listening and can hear us chuckling, any disapproval notwithstanding, at his transgression.

"This Is Just to Say" asks to be taken as a verse letter (or Post-It note). The title of one of Ezra Pound's best-known poems *tells* us it's epistolary.

THE RIVER-MERCHANT'S WIFE: A LETTER

After Li Po

While my hair was still cut straight across my forehead
I played about the front gate, pulling flowers.
You came by on bamboo stilts, playing horse,
You walked about my seat, playing with blue plums.
And we went on living in the village of Chokan:
Two small people, without dislike or suspicion.

At fourteen I married My Lord you.
I never laughed, being bashful.
Lowering my head, I looked at the wall.
Called to, a thousand times, I never looked back.

At fifteen I stopped scowling,
I desired my dust to be mingled with yours
Forever and forever and forever.
Why should I climb the look out?

At sixteen you departed,
You went into far Ku-to-yen, by the river of swirling eddies,
And you have been gone five months.
The monkeys make sorrowful noise overhead.

You dragged your feet when you went out.
By the gate now, the moss is grown, the different mosses,
Too deep to clear them away!

The leaves fall early this autumn, in wind.
The paired butterflies are already yellow with August
Over the grass in the West garden;
They hurt me. I grow older.
If you are coming down through the narrows of the river Kiang,
Please let me know beforehand,
And I will come out to meet you
As far as Cho-fu-Sa.

This poem is a translation/adaptation/recasting of a Chinese original. (Any of these alternatives will do, especially since Pound didn't know Chinese; he was working from a preexisting English-language trot.) As letters, verse or otherwise, go, it's a strange one. It doesn't catch its intended recipient up on recent news or express the writer's thoughts or feelings of the day or do any of the other things letters usually do. In fact it's less a letter than, for most of its length, a story, or more precisely a history: a pocket reprise of the wife's entire experience with, and of, her husband. (At the beginning of this section, I listed verse letter and narrative as two subtypes of the poetry of address. This poem combines them.) The poignancy of the wife's story derives in no small measure from her evident need to tell it, which she does from a retrospective distance that suggests she sees her marriage as, if not over, then well on its way to being so.

Prominent among the poem's virtues is its economy. The sixteen or so years of the wife's existence are dispatched in four brief stanzas focused, respectively, on her childhood, her betrothal (and subsequent, "scowling" bashfulness), her acceptance of the marriage (to the point of bliss), and her husband's departure. Each of these epochs in the wife's young life is portrayed via particulars. In the first stanza alone, we have the straight-cut hair, the flower pulling by the gate, the playing of horse on bamboo stilts, the blue plums, the "village of Chokan." . . . Here's a writer taking his own famous advice to "go in fear of abstraction"—though who's to say that the stanza's last line, with its abstract emotions of "dislike" and "suspicion," isn't its most telling.

One could question particular bits of writing in this poem. Something subtler than "sorrowful" could be imagined for the monkeys' noise; do we need the poeticism of "in wind"? doesn't the stab of "they hurt me" render "I grow older" anticlimactic? (I might as soon see "they hurt me" eliminated, which would make more room for "I grow older" to expand affectively.) But I'd rather call out perhaps the best thing in the poem: the wife's offer to come out and meet her husband "as far as Cho-fu-Sa." A close student of the poem once told me that this should be taken to mean very far indeed. But might it not also contain at least a hint of "that far, but no farther"? How the young wife longs to be reunited with her husband—yet on the latter reading she might be communicating enough practicality and/or wariness and/or self-respect to indicate that she isn't willing to pursue this longing to *any* length. . . . However one reads it, the ending on "Cho-fu-Sa" demonstrates, like Thomas's on "Gloucestershire" and Keats's on "Darien," the understatedly resonant power of a concluding place-name.

From one of Frost's letters: "When they want to know about inspiration, I tell them it's mostly *animus*." Frost knew his Latin more than well enough to know that *animus* means "inspiration" as well as "hostility," but he was referring in part, or more, to the latter.

Some memorable poems of address are in fact poems of invective. It's considered bad form for such a poem to name its addressee. Yeats refrains from doing so, for instance, in this squib of his:

TO A POET, WHO WOULD HAVE ME PRAISE CERTAIN
BAD POETS, IMITATORS OF HIS AND MINE

You say, as I have often given tongue
In praise of what another's said or sung,
'Twere politic to do the like by these;
But was there ever dog that praised his fleas?

But making his addressee anonymous was the last thing Robert Browning had in mind when he sat down, or reared up, to write his poem "To Edward Fitzgerald" (the same Edward Fitzgerald who so memorably translated "The Rubaiyat of Omar Khayyam"). In 1861, Fitzgerald had written in a letter to a friend that the death of Browning's wife, the poet Elizabeth Barrett Browning, "is rather a relief to me, I must say: no more *Aurora Leighs*. . . . She and her sex had better mind the kitchen and children." Browning discovered this passage many years later in a posthumous edition of Fitzgerald's letters and responded, in 1889, as follows:

TO EDWARD FITZGERALD

I chanced upon a new book yesterday;
I opened it, and, where my finger lay
'Twixt page and uncut page, these words I read—
Some six or seven at most—and learned thereby
That you, Fitzgerald, whom by ear and eye
She never knew, "thanked God my wife was dead."
Aye, dead! and were yourself alive, good Fitz,
How to return you thanks would task my wits.
Kicking you seems the common lot of curs—
While more appropriate greeting lends you grace,
Surely to spit there glorifies your face—
Spitting from lips once sanctified by hers.

For brilliance and singularity *and* animus, this poem is hard to beat. It begins with Browning's shocking—and false—claim that Fitzgerald had "thanked God" Elizabeth was dead. (Fitzgerald had "merely" found her death, in a phrase of unspeakable snarkiness, "rather a relief." Browning's heightening of Fitzgerald's insult is a fusion of poetic license and poetic justice.) *Aye, dead!*: in its bitter realization, this phrase is addressed as much to Browning himself as it is to Fitzgerald. But beyond its emotionality, the phrase also serves as a pivot that directs the poem toward the dizzying, lethal logic of its remainder. Elizabeth, after all, isn't the only one dead; Fitzgerald is too. But—and here comes the poem's key thrust of thought—if Fitzgerald were alive, how might Browning suitably thank him for his appalling words? *Thank* him? The idea puzzles at first, but we quickly discover that "thank" is meant ironically (irony having been introduced in the previous line by the mock-bonhomie of "good Fitz"). "Thanks" in the form of kicking is too "common" a punishment for the "cur" Fitzgerald is. Now comes a line that isn't just puzzling but downright baffling at first: "While more appropriate greeting lends you grace." Grace is the last thing Browning would want to lend Fitzgerald: this much we know, but that's as much as we know, until the poem's final lines clue us in to the "more appropriate" greeting Browning has in mind. Even here, the revelatory goods are withheld until the last moment. "Surely to spit there glorifies" (what?) "your face— / Spitting from lips once sanctified" (how?) "by hers." If you wanted to praise the diction in these lines (the unexpected elevation of *glorifies* and *sanctified*) and/or the music in them (the alliteration of *Surely/spit, glorifies/face*, the assonance of *spitting/lips*), I'd be right there with you. But it's the idea in these lines—the wicked conceptual reversal that transforms spitting, via sanctification, into glorifying—that makes them indelible.

I once took a course on Frost and Thomas Hardy from Joseph Brodsky. He told the class how, as a young poet in Russia, he'd first encountered Frost's work in a Russian translation. I asked him if Frost's distinctive voice came through in it. I didn't see how it could have, that voice being so intimately bound up with English—more specifically, New England-ish—speech rhythms. So I was surprised and a little taken aback by the fierce emphaticness of Brodsky's "Absolutely!"

I also recall the singsong intonation with which Brodsky recited the poems of Frost and Hardy alike. (I've since learned that this intonation, which you can hear in his readings on YouTube, is the default one in Russia for the recitation of poetry.) A poem I especially remember hearing Brodsky read is one by Hardy. How growlingly he ground in the *nothing* in its last line!

IN THE MOONLIGHT

"O lonely workman, standing there
In a dream, why do you stare and stare
At her grave, as no other grave there were?

"If your great gaunt eyes so importune
Her soul by the shine of this corpse-cold moon,
Maybe you'll raise her phantom soon!"

"Why, fool, it is what I would rather see
Than all the living folk there be;
But alas, there is no such joy for me!"

"Ah—she was the one you loved, no doubt,
Through good and evil, through rain and drought,
And when she passed, all your sun went out?"

"Nay: she was the woman I did not love,
Whom all the others were ranked above,
Whom during her life I thought nothing of."

This poem is, of course, a dialogue (another subtype of the poetry of address). Is the "workman" a gravedigger? Not clear but not likely; he seems to be in the cemetery not to dig a grave but to commune with a woman who's already buried there. The workman's interlocutor steps up twice to the plate of interaction—and strikes out both times. First he warns the workman that in staring so fixedly at the woman's grave, he might "raise her phantom." The workman's surprising response could be paraphrased as "I should be so lucky." (The workman's "fool" seems a little harsh: a sign, presumably, of his extreme emotional state.) The interlocutor absorbs the workman's correction and even tries, empathetically, to run with it, saying that the woman was doubtless "the one"—not just one but the one—the workman loved. Whence the workman's second and even more crushing corrective: while the woman was indeed the one, she was the one he *didn't* love; the one (the screw of irony tightens) whom "all the others were ranked above"; the one (the screw receives a further, clinching twist) whom during her life the workman "thought nothing of." Hardy's huge poetic oeuvre is rife with irony of this sort, to the point where it can become predictable and even oppressive. But this poem, in so powerfully epitomizing this irony, inclines one to forgive the obsessive bent that gave rise to it.

(For the obverse of the ironic situation in the poem, see—also a dialogue—Hardy's better-known and grimly funny "Ah, Are You Digging on My Grave?")

One could find fault with some of the writing in "In the Moonlight." *Corpse-cold* is a little blatant. *Good and evil? Rain and drought?* Neither of these trite oppositions seems worthy of the master Hardy was in the main, but then even Hardy couldn't generate over nine hundred poems (many of them fair sized), not to mention the epic verse drama *The Dynasts*, if he was going to take the time to charge every word with brilliance. *All your sun went out* could be criticized not for triteness but for what many commentators see as an awkwardness in Hardy's poetry. This quality is sometimes praised as an earnest of authenticity, sometimes condemned as evidence of ineptness. *All your sun went out* could be advanced in support of either view, whereas the "awkwardness" of the poem's last line—"Whom during her life I thought nothing of"—seems to me an unequivocal virtue. The resistance in its rhythm suggests the wresting of a hard truth from the heart. The line also should give the coup de grâce to the idea (which, if it's still breathing at all, is on life support) that a sentence shouldn't end with a preposition. "Of whom during her life I thought nothing" would be a stylistic catastrophe even if it weren't, in this poem, a metrical impossibility. (This King's English version would also eliminate the poem's close, so audibly relished by Brodsky, on the dyingly assonant **nothing of**.)

An additional word on Brodsky. His poetry in English can seem unidiomatic in spots. (I of course defer to Anna Akhmatova and others as to the brilliance of his poetry in Russian.) And there can be a glibness to his criticism, as manifested for instance in his penchant (which seems to have rubbed off on his friend and fellow Nobelist Derek Walcott) for comparing linear features in the landscape to the lineation of poetry. A particularly dubious example is his likening of the stacked cord of firewood in Frost's "The Woodpile" to a poetic quatrain, a comparison whose facileness is an insult to the Frost who, when he wanted to write about poetry in his poems—"There's so much criticism *in* them, *in* them," he said—did so with an imagination and depth that beggars Brodsky's simplistically pictorial notion. (A case in

SUBJECT AS SOMETHING TO SAY

point would be a line that, in its amalgamation of music, profundity, and wit, is among Frost's greatest: his assertion, in "Directive," that streams up near their high-mountain source are "Too lofty and original to rage.") But whatever my quibbles about Brodsky, there will always be a place in my heart for his open, unstinting, and, for a nonnative English speaker, remarkable love of Frost and Hardy. I'll be forever in his debt—as perhaps you now are too—for calling attention, in his teaching of "In the Moonlight," to a wonderful poem I might otherwise have overlooked.

Another poem in dialogue (of a kind) is "Heaven," by George Herbert. There was a vogue for echo poems of this sort in the sixteenth and seventeen centuries. ("Heaven" appeared in Herbert's collection *The Temple* in 1633.)

O who will show me those delights on high?
            Echo.   I.
Thou Echo, thou art mortall, all men know.
            Echo.   No.
Wert thou not born among the trees and leaves?
            Echo.   Leaves.
And are there any leaves, that still abide?
            Echo.   Bide.
What leaves are they? impart the matter wholly.
            Echo.   Holy.
Are holy leaves the Echo then of blisse?
            Echo.   Yes.
Then tell me, what is that supreme delight?
            Echo.   Light.
Light to the minde: what shall the will enjoy?
            Echo.   Joy.
But are there cares and businesse with the pleasure?
            Echo.   Leisure.
Light, joy, and leisure; but shall they persever?
            Echo.   Ever.

40

SOME POEMS THAT SAY BY ADDRESSING

This Q&A between speaker and Echo is conceptually divisible into three parts. In the first, which comprises just the first question and answer, the Echo says it's he (or maybe He) who will show the speaker "those delights on high." In the next part—the next three questions and answers—the speaker skeptically interrogates the Echo's qualifications for the job. Surely you're (merely) mortal, suggests the speaker. Not so, says the Echo. But weren't you born "among the trees and leaves" and therefore, like anything born of this world, in *fact* mortal? Well, says the Echo slyly, I was born among leaves, at least. The speaker asks if there are any leaves "that still abide," that is, that *aren't* mortal. "Bide," the Echo responds, that is, bide your time, be patient. But the speaker isn't in a patient mood: what kind of leaves is the Echo talking about? Stop being coy; "impart the matter wholly." The Echo puts a stop to this line of questioning, and an end to the speaker's skepticism, with the most satisfactory of answers: "Holy" leaves, that is, leaves of Scripture. The Echo's bona fides as a heaven maven having been established, the speaker presses the Echo, in the poem's third conceptual section, for some specifics on heaven's delights. The Echo's responses, far from being coy, now have a transparent simplicity that's part and parcel of the vision on offer.

The echo technique in the poem is at its most brilliant when applied to bi-syllabic words: the detaching, for example, of *bide* from *abide,* and the *wholly/holy* pair, in which these homonyms convey first the speaker's impatience with the Echo and then the Echo's quashing-at-a-stroke of same. *Pleasure/leisure* adds a sonic dimension to the semantic connection between these words. And then there's the poem-concluding *persever/ever.* This heart-stoppingly beautiful close is of a kind Herbert had something of a patent on, one whose resonance expands outward like the sound of a gong or ripples spreading concentrically on the surface of a pond. (We've already seen an example in the *something understood* that closes "Prayer [I].") It's hard enough to achieve such an ending under any circumstances; to do so under the constraints of the echo technique, as Herbert does in "Heaven," is borderline unaccountable.

A huge portion of the poetry of address is narrative. Poems that tell stories go back a long way—at least as far back as *The Iliad* and the Old

Testament, to consider just the Western tradition. I earlier mentioned Ovid's version of the King Midas story. In medieval times, John Gower produced a fine Englishing of it. Gower (1330–1408) is best known, when known at all, as a lesser contemporary of Chaucer, but he had his own winning way with a tale. Here's an excerpt from Gower's "Midas" retelling. The Middle English may make for some jounces in the modern reader's ride but nothing that throws one.

> For he to Bachus thane preide,
> That whereupon his hond he leide,
> It sholde thurgh his touche anon
> Become gold, and thereupon
> This god him granteth as he bad.
> Tho was this king of Frige glad
> And forto put it in assai
> With al the haste that he mai,
> He toucheth that, he toucheth this,
> And in his hond al gold it is,
> The Ston, the Tree, the Lef, the gras,
> The flour, the fruit, al gold it was.
> Thus toucheth he, whil he mai laste
> To go, bot hunger ate laste
> Him tok, so that he moste need
> Be weie of kinde his hunder fede.
> The cloth was leid, the bord was set,
> Al was forth tofore him fet,
> His disch, his coppe, his drinke, his mete;
> Bot whanne he woulde or drinke or ete,
> Anon as it his mouth cam nyh,
> It was al gold, and thane he syh
> Of Avarice the folie.

A striking thing about this narration is its velocity. Nothing is described, fleshed out, or particularized. The tree, leaf, flower, are generic, as are Midas's dish, cup, drink, and meat; both sets of elements

42

are presented with almost dizzying rapidity in a pair of lists. Also notable is the passage's shift of tense. Gower doesn't say, as one would expect in this essentially past-tense narrative, that Midas "touched" things; rather, he "toucheth" (that is, "touches") them. This move lends an immediacy that's heightened by the use of the verb *to be:* "And in his hond al gold it **is**." Not "all gold it becomes" or "turns to"; everything Midas touches simply and suddenly *is* gold. The transformation couldn't be made to seem more magically instantaneous.

For all its brevity, a poem of address by Keats's friend Leigh Hunt could also be called a narrative.

JENNY KISS'D ME

Jenny kiss'd me when we met,
Jumping from the chair she sat in;
Time, you thief, who love to get
Sweets into your list, put that in!
Say I'm weary, say I'm sad,
Say that health and wealth have missed me,
Say I'm growing old, but add,
Jenny kiss'd me.

Strictly speaking, the narration in this poem occupies only its first two lines: the rest is a kind of commentary on the incident recounted. To go by lines 3–4, this commentary is addressed to Time, but the poem's remaining lines are addressed to . . . what? Perhaps an entity more formidable still: a kind of Watcher-in-the-sky who passes judgement on one's nature and achievement. While the defiance of "put that in!" doesn't abate entirely in what follows, it's softened, amid the poet's suggestion of his failings, to a kind of bemused but stubborn pride. The burden of this little masterpiece is perhaps best expressed by Ira Gershwin: "They Can't Take That Away from Me."

Robert Frost told many stories in his poems, but most of them are couched as dramatic monologues (for example, "A Servant to Servants") or dialogues (for example, "The Death of the Hired Man"). Some other, humorous ones are done in ballad-form ("Brown's Descent," for example, or—not entirely humorous—"The Bearer of Evil Tidings"). In "'Out, Out—,'" Frost tells a story in, less commonly for him, a "straight," fiction-like way, though even here he departs from this approach in spots.

> The buzz-saw snarled and rattled in the yard
> And made dust and dropped stove-length sticks of wood,
> Sweet-scented stuff when the breeze drew across it.
> And from there those that lifted eyes could count
> Five mountain ranges one behind the other
> Under the sunset far into Vermont.
> And the saw snarled and rattled, snarled and rattled,
> As it ran light, or had to bear a load.
> And nothing happened: day was all but done.
> Call it a day, I wish they might have said
> To please the boy by giving him the half hour
> That a boy counts so much when saved from work.
> His sister stood beside them in her apron
> To tell them "Supper." At the word, the saw,
> As if to prove saws knew what supper meant,
> Leaped out at the boy's hand, or seemed to leap—
> He must have given the hand. However it was,
> Neither refused the meeting. But the hand!
> The boy's first outcry was a rueful laugh,
> As he swung toward them holding up the hand
> Half in appeal, but half as if to keep
> The life from spilling. Then the boy saw all—
> Since he was old enough to know, big boy
> Doing a man's work, though a child at heart—
> He saw all spoiled. "Don't let him cut my hand off—
> The doctor, when he comes. Don't let him, sister!"
> So. But the hand was gone already.
> The doctor put him in the dark of ether.

He lay and puffed his lips out with his breath.
And then—the watcher at his pulse took fright.
No one believed. They listened at his heart.
Little—less—nothing!—and that ended it.
No more to build on there. And they, since they
Were not the one dead, turned to their affairs.

The felicities come thick and fast in this poem. The *snarled and rattled* in its first line can seem simply a bit (if an effective one) of aural atmospherics, but six lines later we learn, in a revelation of the phrase's descriptive precision, that the saw made these sounds "as it ran light or had to bear a load" respectively. "Making" dust and "dropping" sticks of wood ("stove-length" ones—so we know what this wood will be used for) aren't the first verbs you'd apply to these actions, but you'd be hard put to improve on the aptness of either. The poem's nod to olfaction in the beautiful "Sweet-smelling stuff when the breeze drew across it" is as memorable as anything else in it. The same could be said of those "Five mountain ranges one behind the other / Under the sunset far into Vermont." Also admirable is "those that lifted eyes," a qualification that only *seems* peculiar, in that the eyes of most of those present would have been directed downward to the task at hand. All these strokes in just the first eight lines: a piece of scene setting as economical as it is evocative.

And nothing happened: a clause almost onomatopoeic in its representation of the uneventfulness it describes. "Day was all but done," Frost continues—and then takes *day* for a little spin:

Call it a day, I wish they might have said
To please the boy by giving him the half hour
That a boy counts so much when saved from work.

These lines remind me of a jazz musician's "working" of a motif; Frost might even be criticized for showing his constructor's hand a little too openly in them. But when he proceeds similarly with *supper,* no criticism of the shocking result could be contemplated, let alone leveled:

His sister stood beside him in her apron
To tell them "Supper." At the word, the saw,
As if to prove saws knew what supper meant,
Leaped out at the boy's hand, or seemed to leap—
He must have given the hand. However it was,
Neither refused the meeting.

What *might* be criticized in these lines is "He must have given the hand." Frost was never unwilling to indulge his darker side, but "must have given"? One could believe "it was almost as though" the boy had given the hand, or some such, but in going for the unthinkable here, Frost risks shooting past the plausible. Which makes the characteristically Frostian retreat to ambivalence that follows—"However it was"—seem expedient under the circumstances.

I mentioned that there are spots in this poem that depart from the "straight" narration of fiction. The first of these is the "I" in "Call it a day, I wish they might have said." So a person who was present, not an omniscient narrator, is telling this story. The voice of this person—a speaking voice, not a writing one—can be heard in the outcry of "But the hand!" and "So" (of "So. But the hand was gone already."), a word whose tone is hard to characterize—summary? resigned? a single syllable saying "that's how it was"?—but instantly familiar in the mind's ear. The sound of speech is also perceptible, if perhaps less obviously, in these lines—

Then the boy saw all—
Since he was old enough to know, big boy
Doing a man's work, though a child at heart—
He saw all spoiled.

—as an interruption, a parenthesis, and a resumption ventriloquize a naturalistically hesitant unfolding of utterance.

From here to its conclusion, the poem needs no commentary (certainly no explication). But given my admiration for it, perhaps you'll permit me a cavil regarding its final lines. I've always felt there's something off about "since they / Were not the one dead." One gets the attempt at a killing irony, but might this irony be a little too lethal, too easy and obvious—maybe even a little gratuitously pleasure taking?—in its brutality?

The opening line of a poem by Robert Herrick is far better known than its title.

TO THE VIRGINS, TO MAKE MUCH OF TIME

Gather ye rose-buds while ye may,
Old Time is still a-flying;
And this same flower that smiles today
Tomorrow will be dying.

The glorious lamp of heaven, the sun,
The higher he's a-getting,
The sooner will his race be run,
And nearer he's to setting.

That age is best which is the first,
When youth and blood are warmer;
But being spent, the worse, and worst
Times still succeed the former.

Then be not coy, but use your time,
And while ye may, go marry;
For having lost but once your prime,
You may forever tarry.

This is clearly a poem of address but of a subtype we haven't yet encountered: an injunction. The imperative voice sounds in only three of the poem's sixteen lines, but the whole poem is a piece of forceful advice. Herrick is considerate enough to give arguments for what he's espousing—in fact, these arguments constitute most of the poem—but one doesn't feel he'd be of a mind to entertain objections.

The excellence of this poem can be obscured by its familiarity.

There isn't a syllable of dross in it. The trochee of *Gather* launches it energetically. The "feminine" endings on its odd-numbered lines give it a musical swing. The poem's third stanza is especially admirable. Herrick risks a strong enjambment here, one that, in the context of the poem's prevailingly regular meter, falls somewhere between startling and shocking: "But being spent, the worse, and worst / Times still succeed the former." (Note that the meter forces us to hear *Times* as unaccented: "Times **still** su**cceed** the **for**mer.") But the dire power of what this spot is saying helps carry us over, even as it's heightened by, the enjambment's disruptiveness. It's true that this disruptiveness may reflect, as much as anything else, the difficulty of finding a rhyme for *first*—

> That age is best which is the first,
> When youth and blood are warmer;
> But being spent, the worse, and worst
> Times still succeed the former.

—which only goes to show that a formal constraint can force even a masterful poet beyond his or her customary brilliance.

Injunctions are grounded in authority, and no poet was, or at least can sound, more authoritative than Emily Dickinson. As a member of a high-status New England family, Dickinson was to some extent born to this quality. (It may have been bequeathed more particularly by her strict and formidable father, a man whose heart, she said, was "pure and terrible.") In one of her better-known poems, Dickinson opens with an injunction and then, like Herrick in "To the Virgins," devotes the rest of the poem to arguing for its validity.

> (1263)
>
> Tell all the truth but tell it slant—
> Success in Circuit lies
> Too bright for our infirm Delight
> The Truth's superb surprise

48

As Lightning to the Children eased
With explanation kind
The Truth must dazzle gradually
Or every man be blind—

You could accuse this poem's first four lines of a certain conceptual instability, unless you're of a mind to praise them for same. Having been told to tell the truth "slant"—that is, obliquely, at an angle—we're then told that success lies in "Circuit": in going *around* the truth. This geometrical inconsistency doesn't trouble Dickinson, which doesn't mean it might not trouble us. Lines 3–4 may also cause a little knitting of the brows, at least initially. *Bright* isn't the most natural descriptor for the power of a surprise (*infirm* is an even odder, if intriguing, descriptor for *Delight*), though since Dickinson is talking about that most illuminating source of surprise, the Truth, *bright* can also be seen in this context as the aptest of descriptors. The idea of Truth's brightness launches Dickinson, furthermore, on a flight of imagination and diction as inspired as any in her poetry (which is to say, in poetry). Can there be a more magnificent simile than her likening of the "slant" communication of Truth to the anodyne explaining of lightning to frightened children? The wonderful word choice at this simile's heart, *eased,* is succeeded by the brilliantly paradoxical conjunction of *dazzle* with *gradually.* Such fireworks of diction can do little but subside, though what they give way to—"Or every man be blind"—is beautifully lapidary.

Dickinson's authority is most often encountered not in injunctions but in another subcategory of poems of address: proclamations of a general truth. "Much madness makes divinest sense," "There is a pain so utter," "A light exists in Spring," "There is no Frigate like a book": Dickinson was always more than ready to tell us how it is. In his essay "An Apologie for Poetrie," Philip Sidney famously said, "The poet affirmeth not" (itself an affirmation—that is, an assertion—of course, but, having been committed in prose rather than poetry, presumably excusable). If Dickinson knew Sidney's dictum, her acquaintance with it doesn't seem to have given her pause. Her poem that begins "Success is counted sweetest" (#112) "affirmeth" a truth so central to her psyche that she returned to it more than once in her work.

> Success is counted sweetest
> By those who ne'er succeed.
> To comprehend a nectar
> Requires sorest need.
>
> Not one of all the purple Host
> Who took the Flag today
> Can tell the definition
> So clear of victory
>
> As he defeated—dying—
> On whose forbidden ear
> The distant strains of triumph
> Burst agonized and clear!

"To *comprehend* a nectar"? Shades of "infirm delight": If you don't acknowledge the strained strangeness that can sometimes attend Dickinson's matchless way with words, you're cutting her a break. A touch of this strangeness also attaches to the defeated soldier's "forbidden ear." In a literal sense, it's the soldier, not his ear, that's "forbidden" from victory—in fact, it's precisely his ear that's *not* forbidden from it, in that the "strains of triumph" are audible to him—and yet we have no trouble understanding what Dickinson is trying to say. The very illogic of *forbidden ear* lends the phrase, and the poem, a salutary electricness, rather as a short circuit arcs across wires that shouldn't be touching.

A similar cross circuiting occurs when Dickinson says that the strains of triumph "burst agonized and clear" on the defeated soldier's ear. Isn't it the soldier, not the strains, who would be "agonized"? That said, the voltage of *this* illogic, if that's what it is, is even higher than that of *forbidden ear,* lending its considerable charge, intensified by one of Dickinson's rare exclamation points, to the poem's conclusion. With all this talk of peculiarities of diction, it's worth pointing out that Dickinson was perfectly capable of the most straightforward strokes:

"As he defeated—dying—," for instance. Was *dying* tossed in to fill out the meter? Possibly—which doesn't prevent it from coming across as a moving almost-interjection. Also moving is the way *dying's* strong-to-weak rhythm echoes, like the second of two terminally reversed heartbeats, the rhythm that ends *defeated* just before.

Sometimes the poetic "affirming" of a general truth is not merely authoritative but vatic. A paradigm case is a little brick of a passage by someone who might have answered as readily to "prophet" as "poet":

> What is it men in women do require?
> The lineaments of Gratified Desire.
> What is it women do in men require?
> The lineaments of Gratified Desire.
> (From "Several Questions Answered")

We noted some oddities of diction in Dickinson. This passage, by William Blake, offers such an oddity of its own—the ascription of lineaments to desire (meant to be understood, presumably, as the ascription of lineaments to the visible object of that desire)—but what's more peculiar about the passage is the brute primitiveness of its form. What more to say about this passage? (Which itself says something about it.)

The transmission of a general truth in Philip Larkin's "Talking in Bed" is diametric to that in "Several Questions Answered," as subtle and involute as the latter is brusque and blunt.

> Talking in bed ought to be easiest,
> Lying together there goes back so far,
> An emblem of two people being honest.
>
> Yet more and more time passes silently.
> Outside, the wind's incomplete unrest
> Builds and disperses clouds in the sky,
>
> And dark towns heap up on the horizon.
> None of this cares for us. Nothing shows why
> At this unique distance from isolation

> It becomes still more difficult to find
> Words at once true and kind,
> Or not untrue and not unkind.

The bleakness of the general truth asserted in this poem—that a couple in bed find it "still more difficult" to talk honestly to each other—is worthy of Larkin's signal influence, Hardy. Also Hardy-esque is this truth's ironic counterintuitiveness. In saying that "nothing shows why" talking in bed is especially hard, Larkin is tacitly acknowledging that a "why" is called for.

As fine as this poem is—one of the best short poems by one of the last century's best poets—I find myself querying a few things in it. Though the scene "outside" is painted beautifully, one may sense a poet thinking his poem needs *something* visual in it. . . . The existential dourness of the follow-on observation—"None of this cares for us"—can seem a little reflexive (as can our probable nodding at it). One might also question the little shuffle-step from the *none* of "None of this cares for us" to the *nothing* of "Nothing shows why." The implied connection between the two is weak to the point of nonexistence: a sleight of hand whose deftness doesn't make it any less a trick.

Yet the flaws of "Talking in Bed," if that's what they are, pale in the face of its virtues. The poem's first four lines are admirably direct and eloquent in evoking, even as they question, an ease of communication one would think exists. (A different—very different—poet might have advanced the proposition that talking in bed *is* easiest.) One bows one's head before the delicate tact of "not untrue and not unkind." Best of all may be Larkin's positioning of couples at a "unique distance from isolation." He here goes beyond bleakness into a tragic vision of human connection in futile flight from its impossibility. Even the closeness of a couple is, on this view, only a departure, not an escape, from aloneness.

I said that "Talking in Bed" delivers its general truth subtly. I haven't yet mentioned the aspect of the poem that bears most directly on this point: that it actually delivers *two* general truths. The poem's main truth statement—that

At this unique distance from isolation
It becomes still more difficult to find
Words at once true and kind,
Or not untrue and not unkind.

—is preceded by, and logically enclosed within, the truth statement
that "Nothing shows why" it's true. This nesting of statement-within-
statement yields a kind of verbal perspective in which a statement in
the foreground (talking in bed is difficult) is deepened by a statement
in the background (this difficulty is inexplicable).

As noted earlier, a great many poems of address are narratives. A
great many others are meditations. These can be addressed to the
speaker's self—when such poems are spoken by characters in a verse
play, we call them soliloquies—or to one or more others. In either case,
they enact a train of thought. Here's an example by Thomas Hardy:

HAP

If but some vengeful god would call to me
From up the sky, and laugh: "Thou suffering thing,
Know that thy sorrow is my ecstasy,
That thy love's loss is my hate's profiting!"

Then would I bear it, clench myself, and die,
Steeled by the sense of ire unmerited;
Half-eased in that a Powerfuller than I
Had willed and meted me the tears I shed.

But not so. How arrives it joy lies slain,
And why unblooms the best hope ever sown?
—Crass Casualty obstructs the sun and rain,
And dicing Time for gladness casts a moan. . . .
These purblind Doomsters had as readily strown
Blisses about my pilgrimage as pain.

So *nothing* had it in for me, says the poet, who would have felt better—
purest Hardy, this—if something, or Something, had: his painful "pil-

grimage" was simply luck of the draw. (I've known this poem a long time, but only now does it occur to me that its crushing burden is akin to that of a poem I've known even longer: Frost's "Design," in which a ghastly little tableau—a dead white moth in the clutches of a white spider on an albino flower—moves the poet to muse, "What but design of darkness to appall?— / If design govern in a thing so small.") Hardy wrote "Hap" when he was twenty-six, but his stylistic signatures are already in place: the "awkwardness" ("From up the sky," "Power-fuller," "But not so"), the penchant for odd and/or antiquated words (*unblooms, purblind, strown*), and the resort to words whose oddness consists only in being oddly and wonderfully right (*clench, meted, casts*). All these earmarks of originality presumably help explain why this classic was first published not when it was written—no magazine would take it—but thirty-two years later, in Hardy's first book of poems.

"Hap" seems addressed as much to Hardy himself as to anyone else. Other meditative poems seem directed more outward, more to the reader or a public of readers. Some of the finest of these are too long to be considered here—Wordsworth's "Tintern Abbey" and "Immortality" ode come to mind—but there are also superb shorter examples. In Yeats's "An Irish Airman Foresees His Death," the eponymous speaker—an acquaintance of Yeats, Major Robert Gregory—ponders his likely end in a kind of testament or declaration:

> I know that I shall meet my fate
> Somewhere among the clouds above;
> Those that I fight I do not hate
> Those that I guard I do not love;
> My country is Kiltartan Cross,
> My countrymen Kiltartan's poor,
> No likely end could bring them loss
> Or leave them happier than before.
> Nor law, nor duty bade me fight,
> Nor public man, nor cheering crowds,
> A lonely impulse of delight
> Drove to this tumult in the clouds;

I balanced all, brought all to mind,
The years to come seemed waste of breath,
A waste of breath the years behind
In balance with this life, this death.

Talk about a poem made of iron! Its principles of construction are adhered to with extraordinary consistency. For the first twelve of its sixteen lines, it marches along in what might be called "conceptual couplets": "conceptual" in being defined not by rhyme—the rhyming is in *four*-line units: ABAB CDCD and so on—but by thought. The first of these couplets declares something—the airman's foreknowledge of his death—on which the entire rest of the poem will expand. The succeeding four conceptual couplets sustain, remarkably, a constructive principle *within* each couplet: the first line (for example, "Those that I fight I do not hate") receives a continuation in the second that's syntactically parallel ("Those that I guard I do not love"). I don't know which is more impressive in this stretch of the poem, the virtuosity or the discipline.

The poem's soldierly progress is reinforced by its adherence to perfect rhyme—unusual for Yeats, with his penchant for off-rhyming—and its unadorned diction: no verbal fanciness or frippery here. (Well, almost none: in the poem's only even remotely "poetic" line, we find *drove* taking on extra power in having no object and encounter, in the exciting *tumult,* the poem's only word of even the slightest elevation.) Yeats doesn't deviate from his conceptual coupleting until the last four lines, and when he does, it's only to effect a *tightening* of the constructional reins. This is accomplished via a chiasmus, or reversal of order: the third and fourth of these lines conceptually mirror the second and first respectively, a pattern that embodies the "balance" the lines speak of:

I balanced all, brought all to mind,
The years to come seemed waste of breath,
A waste of breath the years behind
In balance with this life, this death.

(There's even, it boggles the mind to realize, a chiasmus within this chiasmus: the second line's "The years to come | waste of breath" is reversed in the third line's "waste of breath | the years behind.") In rounding on themselves, these last four lines provide a kind of closure to the poem, even as they open it up by shifting its movement from what until now has been a forward march of declaratives to more of a semi-hypnotic circling of utterance and thought.

When I was in my teens, I didn't think much of poetry: too much flora and—this shows how profound my benightedness was—too easy to write; just string some words like *crystal* and *gossamer* together and there you had it. But one poem, which I encountered in high school, was a different matter. It didn't turn me around on poetry overall— that wouldn't even begin to happen until a few years later, when I stumbled on Randall Jarrell's wonderful appreciations of Whitman and Frost—but the poem struck me as a cut so far above that it didn't even count as an exception; it seemed, rather, like the sole representative of a separate, superior species. Only now, as we tour the realm of poems of address, does it occur to me that this poem inhabits it. Add the fact that it's a love poem (surely the ur-type of all poems of address) and that we've yet to consider such a poem, and you'll understand my wanting to end this section with a look at John Donne's "A Valediction: Forbidding Mourning."

As virtuous men pass mildly away,
    And whisper to their souls to go,
Whilst some of their sad friends do say
    The breath goes now, and some say, No:

So let us melt, and make no noise,
    No tear-floods, nor sigh-tempests move;
'Twere profanation of our joys
    To tell the laity our love.

Moving of th' earth brings harms and fears,
    Men reckon what it did, and meant;

But trepidation of the spheres,
    Though greater far, is innocent.

Dull sublunary lovers' love
    (Whose soul is sense) cannot admit
Absence, because it doth remove
    Those things which elemented it.

But we by a love so much refined,
    That our selves know not what it is,
Inter-assured of the mind,
    Care less, eyes, lips, and hands to miss.

Our two souls therefore, which are one,
    Though I must go, endure not yet
A breach, but an expansion,
    Like gold to airy thinness beat.

If they be two, they are two so
    As stiff twin compasses are two;
Thy soul, the fixed foot, makes no show
    To move, but doth, if the other do.

And though it in the center sit,
    Yet when the other far doth roam,
It leans and hearkens after it,
    And grows erect, as that comes home.

Such wilt thou be to me, who must,
    Like th' other foot, obliquely run;
Thy firmness makes my circle just,
    And makes me end where I begun.

Donne wrote this poem before leaving on a trip to the Continent. One imagines him presenting it to its presumed addressee, his wife, Ann, before departing—and her being moved by it to forgive him at least one sort of straying. I'll forgo a discussion of the poem's famous closing "conceit": its super-ingenious, extended comparison of the traveling speaker and his lover back home to the feet of a draftsman's compass. I'm as in awe of this marvel as anyone, but you've probably heard plenty about it elsewhere.

I'd rather note, first, the poem's overall subject. One imagines Donne saying some comforting words to Ann on the eve of his departure, as so many have done in similar circumstances and, unlike so many, having a light click on in his head: here was something that something could be made of poetically. The premise of "A Valediction" has a simplicity that allows it to serve as a kind of spine supporting manifold elaboration. And it's in this elaboration that the poem principally lives: a series of comparisons that, just on the concept level, is exhilarating to contemplate. Donne successively likens his and Ann's ideally unbemoaned parting to the quiet dying of virtuous men, to the movement—"trepidation"—of the planets (of far greater magnitude than the quaking of *this* world yet, unlike an earthquake, utterly silent), the "breachless" expansion of beaten gold (I recently read, to my astonished dismay, that this sublime image was "heavily criticized" by T. S. Eliot as "not being based on a philosophic theory")—culminating, of course, in the comparison to the compasses.

Like a couple of other poems of address we've looked at, this one starts with an injunction: "let us melt, and make no noise, / No tear-floods nor sigh-tempests move." But as in those poems, an imperative quickly gives way to persuasion, though where those other poems (by Dickinson and Herrick) persuaded via argument, this one persuades less instrumentally, through the seductive magic of its comparisons. There's magic as well in the way these comparisons are expressed. Word music is manifest throughout, nowhere more beautifully than in the voluptuous linguals of *Dull sublunary lovers' love,* the musical equal—at least—of Tennyson's famous *murmuring of immemorial elms.* The gorgeousness of this line may lead one to overlook and/or undervalue a different sort of beauty in the immediately succeeding ones: that of the Möbius strip Donne wreathes in saying that the sensual can't bear separation since separation eliminates the sensual. (That *wreathes* reminds me of something ... of Coleridge's saying, in a four-liner whose compression gives even Dickinson's a run for its money, that Donne could "wreathe iron pokers into true-love knots." Speaking of compression, consider Donne's derision here of a love "whose soul is sense": a phrase that were it to be dropped into water would blow up into something like "the essence of which is sense, which is a poor excuse for a soul.")

Beautiful in yet a third way—perhaps the purest of them, a beauty of unadorned eloquence—is the next stanza's contrasting of a merely sensual love to the sort that obtains between Donne and Ann:

> But we by a love so much refined,
>   That our selves know not what it is,
> Inter-assured of the mind,
>   Care less, eyes, lips, and hands to miss.

In the first two of these lines, it's as though the poet has been humbled into the most direct expression, in the simplest words, of a love that has been "refined" (partly in the chemist's sense?) beyond recognition. The third line briefly lets down the stanza's guard against polysyllables but only to admit the wonderful coinage of *inter-assured*. That such writing is brought off in rhyme lends it not only euphony but rhyme's intrinsic tinge of the miraculous.

Among all of this poem's coups, a line in the next stanza, "Like gold to airy thinness beat"—the one Eliot singled out for condemnation—is maybe my favorite thing in "A Valediction." That hyperbolic *airy* seems especially wondrous: no metal can be beaten *that* thin.

The "gateway" poem for the young Billy Collins was, as in my own case, one of Donne's: "The Flea." It's always risky to place a bet against the inimitable and in some ways unsurpassable Collins—and "The Flea" is just a brilliant, brilliant poem—but if it's all right with the house, I'll keep my money on "A Valediction."

༅

Here's a list of the poems we've considered, in the order we've considered them.

SAYING BY EXPRESSING

Title	Author	Subject
Fragment 35	Sappho	A fit of passion
Odi et Amo	Catullus	A coexistence of hate and love
(Thou art indeed just, Lord, if I contend)	Hopkins	Despair at a drought-stricken life
(I'm in Love With) A Wonderful Guy	Hammerstein	Infatuation
from Song of Myself	Whitman	Elation, cosmic sized

SAYING BY EVOKING

Title	Author	Subject
The Eagle	Tennyson	An eagle and its surround
Composed upon Westminster Bridge, September 3, 1802	Wordsworth	A prospect of London
Miniver Cheevy	Robinson	Miniver Cheevy
Those Winter Sundays	Hayden	The poet's father, touching on the poet too
from (The Shield of Achilles)	Homer, Pope	Achilles' shield (ekphrasis)
Adlestrop	Thomas	A moment at Adlestrop
Leda and the Swan	Yeats	A moment in mythology
On First Looking into Chapman's Homer	Keats	A moment in the development of the poet's mind
Prayer (I)	Herbert	The concept of prayer
(The Love a Life can show Below) #673	Dickinson	An ineffable "diviner thing"

SAYING BY ADDRESSING

Title	Author	Subject
The Pasture	Frost	A visit to a pasture (direct address)
This Is Just to Say	Williams	Those plums (direct address—verse note)
The River-Merchant's Wife: A Letter	Pound	A marriage (direct address—verse letter)
To a Poet Who Would Have Me Praise Certain Bad Poets, Imitators of His and Mine	Yeats	Insincere praise (direct address—invective)
To Edward Fitzgerald	Browning	Fitzgerald's unspeakable words (direct address—invective)
In the Moonlight	Hardy	A graveyard scene (dialogue)
Heaven	Herbert	Heaven (dialogue)
from Confesio Amantis	Gower	King Midas (narrative)
Jenny Kiss'd Me	Hunt	A priceless moment (narrative in miniature)
"Out, Out—"	Frost	That buzz saw tragedy (narrative)
To the Virgins to Make Much of Time	Herrick	Carpe diem (injunction)
(Tell all the Truth but tell it slant) #1263	Dickinson	Guidance on the communication of truth (injunction)
(Success is counted sweetest) #112	Dickinson	Deprivation-compensation (statement of a general truth)
from Several Questions Answered	Blake	What men and women require (statement of a general truth)
Talking in Bed	Larkin	Difficulty of doing so (statement of a general truth)

SAYING BY ADDRESSING (*continued*)

Title	Author	Subject
Hap	Hardy	Indifference of the universe (meditation)
An Irish Airman Foresees His Death	Yeats	Thoughts on his likely fate (meditation)
A Valediction: Forbidding Mourning	Donne	Persistence of a higher love (direct address—love poem)

Even a much larger selection couldn't begin to be comprehensive about the realm of subjects in poetry. Surveying this realm is like probing the outdoors at night with a flashlight. We direct the beam here and see a tree trunk. We point it there and see some ferns. Then a boulder, a rabbit. . . . Of course there will always be far more missing from, than present in, this gradually populating picture of so enormous a surround. But as more of that surround's elements are illuminated, its entirety becomes progressively more inferable. In aiming some beams at the landscape of subjects, I hope I've given at least a slight suggestion of its variousness and vastness.

2

Why Subjects?

In a footnote somewhere, I once saw, amid a waving off of Frost's admittedly small and haphazard body of critical prose, the admission that it did contain some interestingly "gnomic" remarks. (Frost's criticism could as easily be said to demonstrate that a critic needn't be voluminous or systematic to be essential.) A disproportionately large number of these remarks are found in "The Figure a Poem Makes." It's as if the poet, aged sixty-four when this essay first appeared, had been saving up a life's worth of gems for it. (He insisted that it be placed at the head of every edition of his collected or complete poems.)

I've already cited the famous claim in "The Figure" that a properly poetic wisdom offers no more—or less—than "a momentary stay against confusion." Frost's follow-up to this claim isn't as familiar, but it deserves to be: that in finding its way toward such wisdom, a poem, "like a piece of ice on a hot stove," should "ride its own melting." Less familiar still, but no less indelible, is Frost's follow-up to this follow-up: that "if you read such a poem a hundred times . . . it will forever keep its freshness as a metal keeps its fragrance." (The fact that the end of this quote is commonly and catastrophically misprinted as "a petal keeps its fragrance" can't have done much for its renown.)

Less noticed than any of these assertions is Frost's serious crack in "The Figure" that "the object in writing poetry is to make all poems sound as different as possible from each other." (Another poet might

63

have said "*be* as different," but "sound as different" reflects Frost's conviction that speech rhythms—"sentence sounds," as he calls them elsewhere—are "the gold in the ore" of poetry.) He goes on to say that the resources of "vowels, consonants, punctuation, syntax, words, sentences, metre are not enough" to establish one poem's difference from another. "We need the help of context—meaning—subject matter. That is the greatest help towards variety."

This argument is worth pausing over. If variety is "the object" in writing poetry and if "subject matter" is "the greatest help towards variety," Frost would seem to be saying that subject matter is the aspect of poetry that's most central to it. And who's to say it isn't? If there's a problem with Frost's view of subjects, it may be that he understates their importance. Subjects can give poems more than variety. And they can benefit not just poems but poets and the art of poetry in general. This chapter is a case for subjects from these several perspectives.

SOME THINGS A SUBJECT CAN GIVE A POEM

Coherence

Contemporary poetry can be a tough place for coherence. Some of today's most prominent poets believe poetry should aim for a mimesis of the mind's less ruly ways. The poet-critic Stephanie Burt, for example, approvingly evokes a poetry (John Ashbery's) that "leaps, as a person's thoughts do, from topic to topic, and . . . lacks, as real people usually lack, a single story line or motive that defines it."

A cousin of this view has been around forever, if you view 1921 as the dawn of time. That's when T. S. Eliot famously argued for difficulty in modern poetry. "Our civilization comprehends great variety and complexity," he wrote, which "playing upon a refined sensibility, must produce various and complex results." Paul Muldoon recently updated this claim: "A world that is complex requires a poetry that is complex; a world that is somewhat incoherent may actually demand a poetry that is itself incoherent." (On this sort of logic, which the poet-critic Yvor Winters long ago identified as a "fallacy of imitative form," a poem about boredom should be boring.)

Poems that simulate the mind's scattered side are currently being written by many poets. It's hard to take even a few steps these days without stumbling on such a poem—one by Lewis Warsh called "Econoline," for instance, which I encountered just this morning on a poem-of-the-day website. Here's a characteristic stanza from it:

> Belief in a weight-loss program
>
> is half the battle. Like when you get
>
> down on your knees and pray for rain.
>
> The train was derailed and the detainees
>
> filled the station. Is it possible to defecate
>
> in the corner of a cage?

Stephanie Burt has applied an influential label to poetry that hopscotches in this way: "elliptical."

Are many people writing such poems? You'd think so, to go by the sort of poetry that predominates in the literary magazines. A statistical confirmation of this impression is beyond both the scope of this book and its author's inclination to diligence. I'll offer, instead, some supporting testimony: not of the most recent vintage but not so old as to be inadmissible. In 2010, the poet Tony Hoagland wrote that the "most prevalent poetic representation of contemporary experience" was "the mimesis of disorientation by non sequitur. Just look into any new magazine. The most frequently employed poetic mode is the angular juxtaposition of dissonant data, dictions, and tones, without defining relations between them." A few years later, the poet Joshua Mehigan was still seeing a domination of poetry by what Hoagland had called a "mimesis of disorientation." In carrying out a project that required him to read thousands of pages of new, unpublished work, Mehigan was sobered to find most of it characterized by "a relentless infatuation with whimsical discontinuity. . . . Non sequiturs abound, in two main flavors, quirkily funny and very—so very—serious." As

I write, roughly a decade after Hoagland offered his take on current poetic modes, things don't seem to have changed much. Poems that make a nod (or more) to coherence certainly have their place in the scene, but my sense is that they still constitute the lesser part of what's published, especially in the more au courant journals.

Elliptical poetry isn't the only kind that traffics in discontinuity these days. There's also what's become known, per its practitioners' term for it, as "Language" poetry. As with elliptical poetry, Language poetry's lack of coherence is intentional, but the intent that drives it is different. Where elliptical poets are trying to say something about the mind—that it's a kind of Mixmaster—Language poets are trying to say something about . . . language: that it's problematically imprecise. (You'd think a poet of any description would be especially impressed with how un-cannily precise language can be.) Many Language poets see an im-precision of language as allowing words to be co-opted by power and bent to its ends. Hard to argue with that, unless it's to say that even if language were perfectly precise, power, being power, would bend words to its ends anyway.

If one accepts, or at least entertains, our working definition of *subject* as "something to say," one might ask if elliptical or Language poems can even have a subject. Some would hold, reasonably, that at least ellip-tical poems can, in that such poems are always saying something about, whatever else, the vicissitudes of consciousness. (Ashbery suggests as much in commenting on his own poetry in the encyclopedia *Contemporary Poets:* "There are no themes or subjects in the usual sense, except the very broad one of an individual consciousness confronting or confronted by a world of external phenomena.") If elliptical poems are saying something about consciousness, however, they're doing so by mimicking this something, not discussing it; they're "about" con-sciousness only in the sense that writing is "about words," that music is "about notes," that air is "about oxygen." (A similar caveat applies to Language poetry, which is less a discussion of language's imprecision than a rigged demonstration of it.)

Whatever discontinuous poetry may or may not have to say, it has plenty of devotees. This isn't surprising: leaving any theorizing about consciousness and/or power to the side, there can be an undeniable electricness to the conceptual, verbal, and imagistic leaps of such poetry. And leaving electricness to the side, such poetry can also have its mysterious, even unaccountable beauties. An astute reader was telling me recently how taken she was with Ashbery's poetry. I asked her what she liked about it. Her way of answering was to utter a few words of his—"These lacustrine cities"—in the sudden, hovering heaven of which each of us gave both of us permission to swoon. (Hoping to preserve whatever respect she may have had for me, I forbore responding with one of my own favorite bits of Ashbery: "Fill your cap with nuts.") I'd even go so far as to say, and I think many lovers of elliptical and/or Language poetry would agree, that the principal pleasures of discontinuous poetry are found *only* in such poetry.

But other pleasures are found only in poetry of a more coherent stripe. And wouldn't an art that knows what's good for itself offer, in its totality, as many pleasures as it can? Lest this question seem merely rhetorical, a reprise of an episode from the recent history of music might be helpful. Every indigenous music in the world is, in a broad sense, "tonal": that is, the various notes in a piece gravitate around a central one. (In Western music, this gravitation was systematized into what we call a "key.") To judge from its global ubiquity, tonality gives pleasure. Which it was left in peace to do for untold millennia until, in Europe, a spirit of experimentation got ahold of it. What followed was a peppering of tonality with a series of what-if's: what if a piece proceeded in an ever-shifting succession of keys, rather than settling into a single one (*Tristan,* anyone?); what if "exotic" scales and chords were employed (as they pioneeringly and preeminently were by Debussy); what if instruments in an ensemble each played in a key of its own (the "bi-tonality," for example, of the famous two-trumpet fanfare in *Petruschka*)—all culminating in the transmutation of these what-if's into a who-says: namely, "Who says music has to be tonal at all?" Arnold Schoenberg's answer to this question—"No one"—led him to a tonality-free, or "atonal" idiom, and thence to a method of "twelve-tone," or "serial," composition whose intent was to systematically rid music of any trace of tonality. The firebrands of serialism (and there were some) seemed to believe tonality could be annulled by fiat. (Pierre Boulez notoriously declared in 1952 that "any musician who has not experienced . . . the necessity for the [serial] language is USELESS.") And from the 1950s through the 1970s, serialism essentially supplanted tonality, if only in the realm of "classical" composition. (Popular music went its blithely tonal way as if serialism had never happened.)

Schoenberg and his successors introduced a new sound world into music, a bequest that no one would want music to be without. (Nor will it be, as long as movies like *Psycho* have soundtracks.) But Schoenberg himself famously averred that "there is still much good music to be written in C major." And tonality never did disappear entirely: like a small mammal in an age of giant reptiles, it persisted in a kind of burrow, resurfacing in the 1980s in such guises as "neo-Romanticism" and, especially, "minimalism." Serialism was still in the picture (and still is) but as only one school among many in the classical realm. (A similar story obtains in painting: representation gives way to abstraction in the decades after World War II, representation then reasserts itself, and representation and abstraction now coexist in a scene in which, to adapt some words of Mao Tse-tung, a hundred flowers are permitted to bloom. In all the arts, this spirit of openness isn't the only thing meant by "postmodernism"—the term is commonly construed as "even *farther out* than modernism"—but this is the meaning of *postmodernism* that may prove the longest lasting and farthest reaching.)

With regard to poetry, what's first called to mind by the tonality-serialism clash is the late-twentieth-century dispute between formal and free verse: how the former was pushed aside by the latter in the 1960s, how it struggled its way back to a modicum of acceptance and visibility, and how it currently lives in comparative peace with its erstwhile antagonist. But the formal–free verse dispute has given way to a new one that pits ellipticism against a more coherent sort of poetry. (Language poetry figures in this dustup as well, though in a supporting, not to say a character, role.) Ellipticists are nowhere near as severe with—what to call them? coherentists?—as the more doctrinaire serialists once were with tonalists, not nearly as inclined to see ellipticism as the next goosestep in a forward march of artistic Progress. That said, ellipticism has left the poetry of coherence lying by a roadside of relative neglect (having tossed it out of the car). At least one prominent ellipticist has gone so far as to suggest that the "preservation," amid our busy lives, of the "drifting experience" induced by ellipticism is "the purpose and promise of poetry." (One wonders if this individual would allow that such less-than-drifty efforts as *The Iliad*, "Western Wind," and "The Second Coming" were at least on the path to poetry's purpose.) My own view is that as music has relaxed in recent years into an acceptance of tonality *and* serialism, poetry would do well to leave room for coherence as well as ellipticism.

This brings us back to subjects. Because a subject helps a poem cohere. Such assistance takes its simplest form in list poetry, like this passage from *Song of Myself:*

> The blab of the pave, tires of carts, sluff of boot-soles, talk of the
>   promenaders,
> The heavy omnibus, the driver with his interrogating thumb, the clank
>   of the shod horses on the granite floor,
> The snow-sleighs, clinking, shouted jokes, pelts of snow-balls,
> The hurrahs for popular favorites, the fury of rous'd mobs,
> The flap of the curtain'd litter, a sick man inside borne to the hospital,
> The meeting of enemies, the sudden oath, the blows and fall,
> The excited crowd, the policeman with his star quickly working his
>   passage to the centre of the crowd,
> The impassive stones that receive and return so many echoes,
> What groans of over-fed or half-starv'd who fall sunstruck or in fits,
> What exclamations of women taken suddenly who hurry home and
>   give birth to babes,
> What living and buried speech is always vibrating here, what howls
>   restrain'd by decorum,
> Arrests of criminals, slights, adulterous offers made, acceptances,
>   rejections with convex lips,
> I mind them or the show or resonance of them—I come and I depart.

Such writing is a structurally simple example of the "orbital" sort of poetry adduced earlier. Its subject—which could be called "sounds of the world"—sits at its conceptual center and exerts a gravitational attraction on all the listed items.

In moving from lists to more complex structures of utterance, orbital poems derive coherence from their subjects in more sophisticated ways. In even so short a poem as "The Eagle," the elements of content are pulled not only gravitationally toward the eponymous raptor at the poem's center but also toward each other by the additional forces of syntax and continuity.

In poems whose path describes less an orbit than a journey—narrative and meditative poems are the two commonest types—coherence is provided by a connectedness from event to event or thought to thought. The degree of coherence in such poems will vary with the strength of the connections. In the realm of narrative poetry, we have, to take an example at an extreme of coherence, that matchless prose poem (as I hereby deem it), Franz Kafka's "The Bucket Rider." (I'd do anything to move you to read this fable's three haunting pages, up to and including refusing to summarize them for you.) The events in this narrative are dreamlike, but each links to the next with Kafka's usual unassailable logic. Whereas the linking is looser, by definition, in episodic works like, to take their granddaddy, *The Odyssey.* The episodes here move from one to the next with little or no narrative necessity; most of them can even be enjoyed singly or in a different order. (The work is held together mainly by the near-omnipresence of its protagonist and, in the background, the goal of his quest.) And then there are episodic poems that don't even try to link their incidents, in which an absence of such linking is part of their point. Notable among these are the so-called I-do-this, I-do-that poems of Frank O'Hara. I find these untethered chronicles as enjoyable as most readers, but if they cohere narratively, so would a recounting of the various things *I* did this afternoon. They're held together, to the extent that they are, by their New York setting and their author's distinctive voice and sensibility.

Meditative poems display a similar range of coherence. A perfectly coherent example, in its clear progression from thought to thought, is Matthew Arnold's "Dover Beach." The poem opens, of an evening, with Arnold inviting his lover to "come to the window," look at the sea, and listen to the "grating roar"

> Of pebbles which the waves draw back, and fling,
> At their return, up the high strand,
> Begin, and cease, and then again begin,
> With tremulous cadence slow, and bring
> The eternal note of sadness in.

Which leads Arnold to the thought that long ago, Sophocles heard in this same, sad cadence "the turbid ebb and flow / of human misery." Which engenders a further thought: that what had long been a source of strength in the face of our misery—a "Sea of Faith" that once was "at the full"—is now audible only in "Its melancholy long withdrawing roar." Upon which crushing realization, Arnold cries out to his lover (remember her?) that they should be "true / To one another!" One wonders if Arnold would have recited this phrase with an emphasis on "one another," as though to aurally suggest a replacement for a trueness to—that is, faith in—God that's no longer possible. What *other* help is left us in a world that "seems / To lie before us like a land of dreams" but which in fact

> Hath really neither joy, nor light, nor love
> Nor certitude, nor bliss, nor help for pain;
> And we are here as on a darkling plain,
> Swept with confused alarms of struggle and flight,
> While ignorant armies clash by night.

A meditation with a looser train of thought is Frost's "Birches." He begins by saying he'd like to think those bent-over birches have been "subdued" by a boy who's been swinging on them. But this fancy has hardly been launched when it's interrupted by the real explanation for the birches' bentness: that they've been bowed by ice storms. This explanation having been introduced, Frost takes it for a beautiful and imaginative spin:

> Often you must have seen them
> Loaded with ice a sunny winter morning
> After a rain. They click upon themselves
> As the breeze rises, and turn many-colored
> As the stir cracks and crazes their enamel.
> Soon the sun's warmth makes them shed crystal shells
> Shattering and avalanching on the snow-crust—
> Such heaps of broken glass to sweep away
> You'd think the inner dome of heaven had fallen.

Until—enough:

> But I was going to say when Truth broke in
> With all her matter-of-fact about the ice-storm
> I should prefer to have some boy bend them.

And on into an account, which, it now becomes clear, the poem was headed for from the first, of exactly how birch swinging is done:

> He always kept his poise
> To the top branches, climbing carefully
> With the same pains you use to fill a cup
> Up to the brim, and even above the brim.
> Then he flung outward, feet first, with a swish,
> Kicking his way down through the air to the ground.

Frost concludes by drawing a moral from this pastime:

> Earth's the right place for love:
> I don't know where it's likely to go better.
> I'd like to go by climbing a birch tree,

And climb black branches up a snow-white trunk
Toward heaven, till the tree could bear no more,
But dipped its top and set me down again.
That would be good both going and coming back.
One could do worse than be a swinger of birches.

It would be stretching things only a little to say that the entire poem, with its ice storm digression that lifts us toward (maybe even to) a heaven of language and image but then returns us to earth, is a figure for the activity it describes.

An approach to poetic meditation that's less—much less—coherent still has been patented by David Kirby. In a 2007 interview with Craig Morgan Teicher, Kirby says that one thing he wants to do in his poems is "portray the mind as it actually works." This may remind us of Stephanie Burt's characterization of Ashbery's poetry as "leaping, as a person's thoughts do, from topic to topic." But Kirby's poetry isn't nearly as labile as Ashbery's; he really does move from "**topic** to topic," whereas Ashbery's poems rarely settle down long enough to proffer a topic even in passing; they mimic the activity less of "the mind" than the brain, to so denominate that organ with respect to its subconscious flickerings. Kirby's poetry therefore seems a more recognizable portrayal than Ashbery's of our mental life as our conscious selves actually experience it.

Here are the first five stanzas of a typically long (fourteen-stanza) Kirby poem entitled "Dogs Who Are Poets and Movie Stars":

As I walk up Sixth Avenue, I pass a dog being dragged
down Eighth Street by its impatient owner,
    and the dog is looking over its shoulder belligerently
at something on the other side of Sixth, so I, too, look
        when I reach the intersection, and I expect to see another dog,

of course, but there's no one there except a woman
with big boobs, so I ask myself, is the dog really a man

who's been turned into a dog for staring too often and too long
at comely women? The ancient Greeks made rather a specialty
        of this sort of thing, didn't they, of seeing to it that chaps

    who didn't behave themselves went through some sort
of metamorphic comeuppance? Do not the wolves
        and lions on Circe's island frighten Odysseus's men
by jumping up on them and wagging their tails
        because they are rogues turned into animals

    by the enchantress? I bet the Eighth Street dog
had been a movie star, because everything I read
        about movie stars suggests they can't control themselves
for more than five minutes. Julianne Moore lives
        on Eleventh, and John, who lives on Twelfth,

    says that if I will take his cairn terrier Henry
for a walk and we run into Ms. Moore, I can talk to her:
        she won't stop for me, but she'll stop to talk to Henry,
and then I can talk to her. But whether or not I run into
        Ms. Moore, I would certainly have to clean up after Henry.

And on the poem goes in this associative fashion: with the movie star
Julianne Moore making Kirby think of Marianne Moore; with a recur-
sion to things canine per a rumination on dog biographies in the "pet
adoption paper"; with a little reflecting on several dogs thus profiled,
including a certain "Josie," which leads Kirby to remark in passing—
here we have a *spitting* image of how the mind "actually works"—that
"my mother's name was Josie"; to the thought, triggered by a dog bio
mention of a dislike of cats, that some dogs are friendlier than others,
a couple of service dogs, for instance, into whose lives Kirby imagines
his way for a bit . . . whereupon it's back to the notion that dogs were
once celebrities, which carries the poem to conclusion.

Burt characterizes our minds' often-wayward movement as a "leaping" from thought to thought. The movement in Kirby's poem is more
like a swinging, Tarzan-like, from vine to vine. This mode of travel *could*

get one to a destination, but it doesn't here; the poem arrives, rather, back in the region where it began. Such a concluding–by–circling back is frequent in Kirby's work, a way of lending closure, if of a somewhat faux persuasion, to poems that are intrinsically, even programmatically, open-ended. (Though if one feels one must close such poems, better a circling back than the tacking on of a boffo—ostentatiously emotional or imagistic—capital *E* Ending. This all-too-common move is reminiscent of a vaudeville comic closing a careening skein of one-liners with a band-enhanced "Ta-da!" of out-flung arms: a gestural punctuation that, given the wayward rush preceding it, seems all the more bogus.)

I'm always happy to encounter a Kirby poem; the wit, nimbleness, and imaginative freedom of "Dogs Who Are Poets and Movie Stars" are characteristic of his work. But Kirby's approach also imposes a constraint on that work. One can be fairly sure a Kirby poem won't have a burden; that its associative moves, for all their pleasures, won't be directed toward a larger point or purpose. True, Kirby may have little or no interest in such directedness: as he says, he wants to "portray the mind as it actually [that is, *un*directedly] works." But while this is a perfectly valid, even laudable literary aim, another thing a poem can do is override the messiness of the mind's "actual" workings by providing a sense—also a feature of our mental life—of a certain order to things. And you don't have to be a completely stuffed shirt to view a poem that essays such an order as having a greater potential for considerableness than a poem that doesn't.

Steadiness

I referred in the previous section to the hopscotching of a poem. The poem in question is recent, but its behavior has an ancestry that goes back at least as far as Eliot-as-collagist:

> London Bridge is falling down falling down falling down
> *Poi s'ascose nel foco che gli affina*
> *Quando fiam uti chelidon*—O swallow swallow
> *Le Prince d'Aquitaine à la tour abolie*

These fragments I have shored against my ruins
Why then Ile fit you. Hieronymo's mad againe.

Such writing has its undeniable thrills but also its associated perils. A recognition of the latter also goes well back: to 1939, at a minimum, when Frost evoked a school of poetic "aberrationists" who traffic in "undirected associations . . . kicking themselves from one chance suggestion to another in all directions as of a hot afternoon in the life of a grasshopper." (For all that these words were penned many decades ago, they seem applicable to any number of poets currently in the throes.) "Theme alone," Frost goes on to say, "can steady us down." A poem of Frost's own is a paradigm case of such steadying.

NEITHER OUT FAR NOR IN DEEP

The people along the shore
All turn and look one way.
They turn their back on the land.
They look at the sea all day.

As long as it takes to pass
A ship keeps raising its hull;
The wetter ground like glass
Reflects a standing gull.

The land may vary more;
But wherever the truth may be—
The water comes ashore,
And the people look at the sea.

They cannot look out far,
They cannot look in deep,
But when was that ever a bar
To any watch they keep?

No "undirected associations" or "chance suggestions" here: this poem is so "steadied down" that it approaches a kind of stasis. Yet it packs a sizable punch. How does Frost manage this? The piece being a poem, one might look for an answer in its language. But the most notable thing about the language here is how ordinary it is. The poem gets by mostly with monosyllables. (And as the poet Elizabeth Spires has observed, mainly generic ones. She cites "Neither Out Far" in questioning the poetry workshop preference for "specific" words: Larkin's "white **steamer** stuck in the afternoon," say, over Frost's simple "ship" that "keeps raising its hull"—both images being, for that, unforgettable.) As with the poem's diction, so with its syntax. The piece proceeds mostly in simple, declarative sentences and clauses (with the notable and powerful exception of the rhetorical question that ends it). You'd think such writing might put a reader to sleep, but its effect here is less soporific than mesmeric. The poem is in fact, in its way, positively gripping—in part *because* of its restraint. There's so little happening on the surface that one suspects something huge to be happening beneath. And as the poet-critic Randall Jarrell tells us in his landmark appreciation of Frost, "To the Laodiceans," something huge is. Jarrell fleshes out this thought in as fine a passage of criticism as this wonderful writer produced:

> We can't look out very far, or in very deep; and when did that ever bother *us?* It would be hard to find anything more unpleasant to say about people than that last stanza; but Frost doesn't say it unpleasantly—he says it with flat ease, takes everything with something harder than contempt, more passive than acceptance. And isn't there something heroic about the whole business, too—something touching about our absurdity? . . . The tone of the last lines—or rather, their careful suspension between several tones, as a piece of iron can be held in the air between powerful enough magnets—allows for this too.

Jarrell is talking about the poem's theme, which could be expressed as something like "humanity's hopeless yet ceaseless search for meaning." But what makes this more than simply a theme is Frost's instantiation of it as a subject: the way people on the beach are forever gazing at the sea. It's the strength of this subject that allows the surface of so effectual a poem to be so quiet. (Frost once penned "quieter" as a self-injunction in the margin of a poem-in-progress.) Even the second stanza's visuals, which might seem intended to enliven things locally, are informed by the poem's master concern. The intermittent visibility of the ship's hull suggests the impossibility of looking "out far"; the reflective glassiness of the "wetter" ground suggests the impossibility of looking "in deep." Not that these visuals lack eye appeal per se: on the contrary, hull and gull take up instant and permanent residence on the retina of one's imagination. The poem would be nothing without its subject, but it wouldn't be nearly as much without these images. I'm reminded of Eliot's reference, in "Little Gidding," to "A condition of complete simplicity / (Costing not less than everything)." Frost's poem earns its simplicity by offering its own sort of everything: a "complete consort," now that I've got "Little Gidding" on the brain, of theme, subject, and imagery "dancing together."

Power

How does a golfer drive a ball three hundred yards? Not with the hands alone, however strong they may be. A golfer's power originates in the large muscles of the legs, butt, and back. These unwind in a coordinated sequence, translating their tremendous force through the levers of the arms and the hinges of the wrists into the whooshing whip of the clubhead.

A poem, like a golf swing, can hit only so hard without the large muscle of a subject. A poem that demonstrates this principle especially well is George Herbert's "The Collar":

> I struck the board, and cried, "No more;
> > I will abroad!
> What? shall I ever sigh and pine?
> My lines and life are free, free as the road,
> Loose as the wind, as large as store.
> > Shall I be still in suit?
> Have I no harvest but a thorn
> To let me blood, and not restore

What I have lost with cordial fruit?
    Sure there was wine
Before my sighs did dry it; there was corn
  Before my tears did drown it.
  Is the year only lost to me?
    Have I no bays to crown it,
No flowers, no garlands gay? All blasted?
       All wasted?
Not so, my heart; but there is fruit,
    And thou hast hands.
Recover all thy sigh-blown age
On double pleasures: leave thy cold dispute
Of what is fit and not. Forsake thy cage,
    Thy rope of sands,
Which petty thoughts have made, and made to thee
Good cable, to enforce and draw,
    And be thy law,
While thou didst wink and wouldst not see.
    Away! take heed;
    I will abroad.
Call in thy death's-head there; tie up thy fears;
    He that forbears
    To suit and serve his need
    Deserves his load."
But as I raved and grew more fierce and wild
    At every word,
Methought I heard one calling, *Child!*
    And I replied *My Lord.*

Within our scheme of "ways of saying," this poem is clearly—even, to
put it in the poem's own terms, fiercely—a poem of address. One could
assign it to the subtype of "meditation," though it can be characterized more precisely still as a rant. It's subject? You could say "religious
stricture," but this answer would be inadequate to the case at hand.
As suggested earlier, the subject of many meditations is more dynamic

than the dictionary definition of *subject* suggests: less an entity than a process. The process here is the speaker's conversion from a chafing under the collar of religion (*collar* in, among other senses, the priestly one) to a salvational submission to it.

Herbert is famous for writing "shaped" poems (one called "The Altar," for example) in which the poem's outline on the page pictures its subject. He does something analogous in "The Collar," in that the speaker's agitated state is reflected in the poem's versification. Its lines vary randomly in meter. They also vary in indentation, with no correspondence, at least no strict one, between the meter of a line and the size of the indent. (It's not uncommon for a poem with varying meter—many by Hardy, for instance—to employ such a correspondence.) And while "The Collar" rhymes throughout, there's no scheme to its rhyming.

The poem's instability of versification abets that more central thing, its "raving" matter. This comes at us in two main thrusts: a series of questions (from "What? shall I ever sigh and pine?" through "All wasted?"), followed, after a reply in the negative ("Not so, my heart"), by a series of sybaritic urgings-to-self (from "Recover all thy sigh-blown age / On double pleasures" down to "Call in thy death's head there; tie up thy fears"). Even as we reel from the rat-a-tat of all this, part of us stands aside to admire its profusion of figures: wind, store, a complex of mainly agricultural images (harvest, corn, bays, and garlands, with a little wine and blood mixed in), on into the cold inanimates of cage, rope of sand (!), cable—capped off by the anti-animate death's-head, whose horrificness is mitigated by the droll request that it be "called in."

I've said that Herbert has something of a patent on endings that resonate outward like the sounding of a gong. The ending of "The Collar" is not only the greatest of these in Herbert but one of the great endings in poetry. The speaker has been working himself into an increasing frenzy of rebellion—and then, in an instant, everything has changed:

But as I raved and grew more fierce and wild
    At every word,

> Methought I heard one calling, *Child!*
> And I replied *My Lord.*

The language of this conclusion, especially that of its final two lines, is remarkably unassuming for a moment of such power. There's a kind of knockout ending whose force comes from the strikingness and/ or energy of its language: the kind epitomized by, say, the last line of Yeats's "Byzantium": "That dolphin-torn, that gong-tormented sea." The power of such a line is largely self-generated, whereas the last lines of "The Collar" derive—better, receive—much of their power from all that's preceded them. The speaker's rant against religion, growing "more fierce and wild / at every word," develops a fast-freight momentum that piles into these lines, where it's converted to a momentous acquiescence in the will of God. To call this transformation instantaneous is to understate its rapidity: by the time the speaker responds to the call of *Child!* he's already acknowledging the caller as *My Lord.* The before-and-after of this conversion is reflected in the dual connotation of both *Child!* ("childish" and "cared for") and *Lord* ("lord-and-master" and "the Lord God").

For a last thought on the ending of "The Collar," I'll return to the image of the golf swing. When you see a really good one, you can't help being impressed by the seeming effortlessness with which the ball is dispatched. Effort is there, but it's been smoothed to inapparency by the perfect timing with which it's applied. This same sort of timing, which tells a comedian exactly when to deliver a punch line, a musician exactly how long to delay a downbeat (Herbert was a virtuoso on the viol), is epitomized by "The Collar's" close.

Distinctiveness

I referred earlier to Frost's assertion that "context—meaning—subject matter" provide "the greatest help" toward variety in poetry.

I find myself thinking, in this connection, of a poem by W. S. Merwin. Merwin's poetry has many virtues, but variety isn't the one that first occurs to me. His poems tend to flow together in my mind as a relatively homogeneous wash of mystical, often ravishing quietness. But one of his poems does stand out for me, and to judge from its popularity, not just for me.

FOR THE ANNIVERSARY OF MY DEATH

Every year without knowing it I have passed the day
When the last fires will wave to me
And the silence will set out
Tireless traveler
Like the beam of a lightless star

Then I will no longer
Find myself in life as in a strange garment
Surprised at the earth
And the love of one woman
And the shamelessness of men
As today writing after three days of rain
Hearing the wren sing and the falling cease
And bowing not knowing to what

Merwin may well have tired of seeing this poem cited and lauded, but he had only himself to blame for its being so. Because he's the one who endowed it with its instantly unforgettable subject: the fact that "every year without knowing it" one passes the anniversary of one's death. There are fine local strokes in the poem, not least its beautiful figures *for* death, but what makes the poem stand out amid the profusion of Merwin's work is its subject. If I had to make a case for a subject's potential to lend distinctiveness to a poem, I'd offer this poem's subject as Exhibit A. (Exhibits B through Z_n would be the diverging roads, Grecian urns, pope's penises, and so on that help earn their poems a unique place in one's mental collection of verse.)

I was interested, by the way, to see the poet-critic Dan Chiasson refer to the subject of "For the Anniversary of My Death" as a "startling idea." It *is* an idea, isn't it. (As distinguished from a person, place, thing, or whatever else a poem's subject may be.) Edgar Degas once told Stéphane Mallarmé, "I'm bursting with ideas for poems." Mallarmé's response? "My dear Degas, poems are made of words, not ideas." One sees Mallarmé's point, but would it be asking too much of a mind to think that a poem can be made of words and ideas alike? I hope not, because many fine poems—Merwin's, for one—are made in this way. Mallarmé is hardly the only poet to question the propriety of ideas in poetry. (A familiar case of such questioning is Archibald MacLeish's "A poem should not mean / but be.") Yet who's to say that what's most likely in a poem to survive the fraying of one's memory, not to mention the windblown sands of time, mightn't be an idea?

Newness

When Pound famously said, "Make it [poetry] new," he was thinking mainly of an innovation in technique: a move from formal verse to free. He never said, "Mission accomplished," but he implied as much in another famous utterance: that breaking the pentameter was "the first heave." He didn't specify any subsequent heaves, but a glance at his *Cantos* suggests that he may have seen one in another technical innovation, fragmentation.

A new technique can certainly lend newness to a poem, but it's not the only thing that can. Another thing that can is a new subject. One might ask if the subject of a poem is ever truly new. It's been said that all poems have one or both of only two subjects: love and death. All poems may in fact treat in some ultimate way of these timeless themes, but themes, not subjects, are what they are. (I earlier proposed a differentiation of theme from subject in the "King Midas" story and in "Neither Out Far nor In Deep." Another example: the theme of "Stopping by Woods on a Snowy Evening" may be a latent wish for oblivion, but its subject is stopping by woods.) When it comes to subjects in their proper, less vastacious sense, their number is closer to infinity than two. Any limit on this quantity is imposed only by the carrying capacity of the universe and/or the mind, the latter being the larger realm, according to Andrew Marvell:

The mind, that ocean where each kind
Does straight its own resemblance find,
Yet it creates, transcending these,
Far other worlds, and other seas.

A good example of a truly new subject is that of the Merwin poem
we've just discussed: the anniversary of one's death. It hardly seems
possible that Merwin's notion hadn't already been come upon, a fact
that makes its unfamiliarity all the more striking. Even Pound at his
most curmudgeonly might have acknowledged that Merwin, in gener-
ating a poem from this subject, had made something new. (Whether he
would have recognized the permanence of this newness is less certain,
though to be fair to him it was he who defined literature as "news that
stays news.")

Not every subject is new, of course. But new ones wouldn't seem
to be in *terribly* short supply. Of the thirty-three poems we looked at
in the previous chapter, thirteen of them have subjects that by my
reckoning are essentially unprecedented (see the table below). Even
with due allowance for imprecision in my accounting (in which I try
to err on the conservative side), this is hardly a negligible proportion.

Title	Author	Subject
Miniver Cheevy	Robinson	Miniver Cheevy
Those Winter Sundays	Hayden	The "lonely offices" of the poet's father
Adlestrop	Thomas	A moment at Adlestrop
On First Looking into Chapman's Homer	Keats	A moment in the development of the poet's mind
This Is Just to Say	Williams	Those plums
To a Poet Who Would Have Me Praise Certain Bad Poets, Imitators of His and Mine	Yeats	Insincere praise

Title	Author	Subject
To Edward Fitzgerald	Browning	Fitzgerald's unspeakable words
In the Moonlight	Hardy	That graveyard scene
Jenny Kiss'd Me	Hunt	A priceless moment
"'Out, Out—'"	Frost	That buzz saw tragedy
Talking in Bed	Larkin	Difficulty of doing so
An Irish Airman Foresees His Death	Yeats	Thoughts on his likely fate
A Valediction: Forbidding Mourning	Donne	Persistence of a higher love in the face of separation

The poems in the previous chapter are admittedly a skewed sample: many of them draw strength from their subjects to an unusual degree. But only in revisiting the full list of these poems did I notice how many of them have subjects that, to repurpose some earlier-quoted words of Frost's, "will forever keep their freshness as a metal keeps its fragrance."

Something to Treat

Say you're going to paint a picture of a tree. You have some decisions to make. Should the rendering be naturalistic? Stylized? Distorted to the point of near-unrecognizability? (Stevens: "A poem should resist the intelligence almost successfully.") What color should the leaves be? Green, after all, hasn't been obligatory since the Fauves, if not earlier. . . . What, if anything, should be in the background? How about endowing the tree with a bird? Would that be a distraction? Just the touch the piece needs? Such questions are questions of treatment.

Say you're going to write a *poem* about a tree. Again, you have some decisions to make. Should it be about a particular kind of tree or just a generic one? (When Hopkins lamented the felling of some trees in "Binsey Poplars," it was important to him, and proper to the poem's elegiac nature, that their species—and their location: Binsey, a village near Oxford—be memorialized. Whereas, consistent with its seeming

a "vague dream-head lifted out of the ground," Frost's "window tree,"
thought to have been a maple growing beside his farmhouse in Derry,
New Hampshire, is left unspecified and unlocated.) Should your poem
about a tree "show" or "tell"? Should it digress? Might the poem, à
la Herbert, call a tree to mind by its appearance on the page? (James
Merrill's "Christmas Tree" is shaped like one.) How about giving your
poem the branching structure of a "tree" of logic? Might the tree be
permitted literally to speak for itself? Again, such questions are questions of treatment. Of course, treatment is only possible in a poem if
there's something to treat—if, that is to say, there's a subject. No subject, nothing to show or tell about, nothing to digress from, nothing
to imitate visually or give voice to.

If a subject affords a poem the possibility of treatment, treatment
can afford a poem a number of additional things. Most simply, it can
imbue a poem with pleasure. In being shaped like its subject, Merrill's
"Christmas Tree" has enjoyably more to it than it otherwise would:
more to ponder, more at which to wonder. So it is with any instance
of treatment. (When Frost said "all the fun's in how you say a thing,"
he had the reader as well as the writer in mind.)

On a deeper level, the treatment of a subject can interpret that subject. Such interpreting might be compared to the effect of harmony
on melody. As a melody makes its way, any chords beneath it progress
per harmony's own ways and laws. Yet while harmony and melody are
separable in theory, in practice they're partners: a chord strummed by
a guitarist "fits" harmonically (that is, is consonant) with the note sung
above it. And relations between harmony and melody aren't just a matter of peaceable coexistence. A chord beneath a melody note imbues
that note with import. An extreme example of such imbuing is Gershwin's "Summertime." Its melody can seem simple, almost folklike,
when detached from its harmony. But add the driftily shifting haze
of that harmony—an addition only a genius could have dreamed of,
let alone effected—and the tune becomes suffused with atmosphere.
The song's lush harmony can be said, in this sense, to interpret its
comparatively spare melody.

In an analogous way, the treatment of a poem's subject can interpret that subject. We've seen this process in action in Herbert's "The Collar," in which the disordered versification of the poem's rant against religion—the couching of it in lines whose meter, indentation, and rhyming are all haphazard—says, as if in as many words, that the rant is the product of an agitated spirit. Or consider another poem by Herbert we looked at, "Heaven." His casting of the poem as a dialogue between a questioner and a teasingly affectionate Echo (aka God) is a way of saying that heaven is ruled by a Being at once remote and approachable—and also, lest we forget, divine. God's ability to answer the speaker's questions by echoing them, another key aspect of treatment in the poem, is a kind of miracle, if of a lesser sort than some He's been known to traffic in.

Herbert's aren't the only poems we've looked at in which treatment interprets a subject. In Whitman's "Song of Myself," the lines' length and freedom from meter bespeak the poet's expansive view of his nature. One feels that the author of this footloose verse is only stating what he sees as the unconceited truth when he says, "I am afoot with my vision." Whereas when Blake asserts, in "Several Questions Answered," that men and women alike require—and, for all he has to say about it, only require—"the lineaments of gratified desire," the clenched jaws of his expression imply a view that's anything *but* expansive. We've also seen Dickinson casting her "diviner thing" not as what it is but, less directly, what it does: an act she performs, in a *prodigy* of indirectness, per a dizzying string of verbs-without-objects. In resorting to this radical measure, Dickinson is saying it both is and isn't impossible to evoke the ineffable in words.

No poem interprets its subject more strikingly via treatment than Elizabeth Bishop's "Visits to Saint Elizabeths" (1956). The poem is a response to the confinement, from 1945 to 1958, of the aging Ezra Pound in Saint Elizabeth's Psychiatric Hospital in Washington, DC. Pound, whose pro-fascist, anti-Semitic radio broadcasts from Mussolini's Italy had led to his indictment for treason, was found unfit for trial by reason of insanity. He was thus spared imprisonment, or even execution, but at the cost of being committed indefinitely to the hospital. Some controversy around this decision notwithstanding, many poets paid visits to him there. One of them was Bishop, who visited Pound a number of times in 1949 and 1950, when she was serving in Washington as Consultant in Poetry to the Library of Congress (a position now known as Poet Laureate).

It's easy to imagine Bishop being moved to write a poem about the sobering situation—and person, and figure—of Pound. What's impossible to imagine—it certainly would have been impossible to predict—is her decision to cast this poem in the form of a nursery rhyme. How in the world did such a thing occur to her? The only answer I can come up with—an entirely speculative one—has Bishop thinking to herself that Pound was sitting in "a madhouse," a thought that triggers a pair of associations: one, via *mad,* to the tradition of the Elizabethan mad song; another, via *house,* to the (singsongy) nursery rhyme "The House That Jack Built," which begins:

1. This is the house that Jack built.

2. This is the malt
    That lay in the house that Jack built.

3. This is the rat,
    That ate the malt
    That lay in the house that Jack built.

Whatever its origins in the crucible of Bishop's creativity, her poem on the subject of Pound's confinement is based, in an extraordinary coup of treatment, *on* "The House That Jack Built." Here, to give a taste of "Visits to Saint Elizabeths," are its first few stanzas:

This is the house of Bedlam.

This is the man
that lies in the house of Bedlam.

This is the time
of the tragic man
that lies in the house of Bedlam.

And following eight successively longer ones, its last:

This is the soldier home from the war.
These are the years and the walls and the door
that shut on a boy that pats the floor
to see if the world is round or flat.
This is a Jew in a newspaper hat
that dances carefully down the ward,
walking the plank of a coffin board
with the crazy sailor
that shows his watch
that tells the time
of the wretched man
that lies in the house of Bedlam.

As is evident from even this little of the poem, there's much to expli-
cate in it and/or much, reflecting Bishop's avowed valuing of "mystery"
in poetry, that may be inexplicable. I'll leave the poem's meanings to
better decryptors than I, and say only, vis-à-vis treatment's power to
interpret a subject, that in casting "Visits to Saint Elizabeths" as a nursery rhyme, Bishop ironizes the poem in a way that makes its burden
all the more terrible . . .

Terrible: As Keats said to his nightingale about *forlorn,* the word
is like a bell that tolls us . . . not back but on, to a final point about
interpreting a subject via treatment. Why does a poet take up a given
subject in the first place? Presumably because the subject "speaks" to
the poet; because it has some interest or import or truth that the poet
feels is worth communicating. In attempting to maximize such communication, poets may interpret their subjects via treatment so as to
emphasize—to throw into relief, to bring into focus, to draw into the
foreground—the significance at their subjects' heart. Thus Herbert,
using haphazard versification to suggest agitation. Thus Whitman,
using unconstrained versification to reinforce an expansive vision.
Thus Dickinson, daring a series of free-floating verbs to evoke the in-
effableness of her "diviner thing." With regard to Bishop, one knows

better than to try to define the interest or import or truth that she found in Pound's sad, if complicated, case. What one *can* say is that in couching this case as a nursery rhyme, Bishop found an extraordinary way to sharpen (and complicate) the sorrow of it all.

SOME THINGS SUBJECTS CAN GIVE A POET

His or Her Voice

As late as his midtwenties—that is, not late at all as these things go— Philip Larkin was still feeling his way into his poetic identity. As is often the case, the process involved an imitating of adored models, first and, to put it charitably, not very well, of Auden:

> There is no language of destruction for
> The use of the chaotic; silence the only
> Path for those hysterical and lonely.
> That upright beauty cannot banish fear,
> Or wishing help the weak to gain the fair
> Is reason for it: that the skilled event,
> Gaining applause, cannot a death prevent,
> Short-circuits impotent who travel far.
>> (From "There is no language of destruction" [1940])

Then, and to little if any better effect, of Yeats:

> Let the wheel spin out,
> Till all created things
> With shout and answering shout
> Cast off rememberings;
> Let it all come about
> Till centuries of springs
> And all their buried men
> Stand on the earth again.
>> *A drum taps: a wintry drum.*
>> (From "All catches alight" [1944])

But when Larkin then takes a tumble for Hardy, whose constitutional dourness must have spoken to his own, he doesn't start sounding like his latest master—though thankfully, he does stop sounding like Yeats: as Larkin himself put it, "the Celtic fever" had "abated." He starts sounding, rather, like this (from the middle of his "Lines on a Young Lady's Photograph Album" of 1953):

My swivel eye hungers from pose to pose—
In pigtails, clutching a reluctant cat;
Or furred yourself, a sweet girl-graduate;
Or lifting a heavy-headed rose
Beneath a trellis, or in a trilby hat

(Faintly disturbing, that, in several ways)—
From every side you strike at my control,
Not least through those disquieting chaps who loll
At ease about your earlier days:
Not quite your class, I'd say, dear, on the whole.

Here's the Larkin we know: now a master himself and one who sounds *like* himself. Why didn't he take on Hardy's voice as he had Auden's and Yeats's? At least in part, I'd submit, because he hadn't taken on Hardy's subject matter (as he'd taken on Auden's and Yeats's). When Hardy looks back at a young woman from his past, he sees her in a phantasmal vision:

As I drive to the junction of lane and highway,
　And the drizzle bedrenches the waggonette,
I look behind at the fading byway,
And see on its slope, now glistening wet,
　　Distinctly yet

Myself and a girlish form benighted
　In dry March weather.
　　　(From "At Castle Botterel")

When Larkin looks back at a young woman from his past, he sees her in some snapshots. Larkin, that is to say, takes his subject from his upper-middle-class world: a world of graduations, trilby hats, disquieting chaps—and photograph albums. It's only natural that when he commits to saying something about this world—his real one—he finds himself saying it in something like his real voice (a voice inflected, to his admirers' everlasting gratitude, with his inimitably droll humor: "reluctant" cat indeed!). On this theory, Larkin may be said to owe the finding of his voice to the finding of his subject matter.

Of course, this is only a theory—which makes me want to recount a kindred experience I know to be actual. In my midtwenties, it was I who was groping toward a poetic identity. Like Larkin at that age, I had a model; unlike Larkin, my model was Frost (though in my youthful pride, I wouldn't have confessed to having any model whatsoever). So it isn't surprising that the poems I was writing back then had country subjects—until it occurred to me that I didn't know the first thing about the country. On recovering from this realization, I started writing poems about New York City, where I'd actually set foot. These poems emerged in a voice that no longer sounded like Frost's (not that it sounded anything like my own). This was progress—stepping away from something was a stride of a kind—but a new problem arose: as damning and/or inexplicable as this may be, there wasn't anything I really had to *say* about New York. This deficit led, for a time, to my not writing any poems at all.

Meanwhile, there was at least one thing I did have to say, if only to get it off my chest: that my lack of poetic production didn't mean I wasn't working on the problem (and that a solution might not be working itself out in me). At some point, it crossed my mind that this could itself be said as a poem. I undertook to execute on the idea—and found that I couldn't. Every stab at the envisioned opus (and there were a number) seemed off somehow, seemed somehow too . . . elevated? I still remember the opening of one of these attempts:

What it never was, was indolence;
Not for an epoch all but given over
To idleness.

After some weeks of this futility, a kind of exhaustion reduced me one afternoon to just blurting out my burden the way I actually would, poetry to the side—whereupon the lines above had morphed into the first sentence of a little poem I *was* able to finish:

NOTICE

Indolent I wouldn't know because
I never was that, forget how
It ever looked. What I was was getting
Ready, and the getting's over now.

This was the first poem of mine that sounded like me, or at least like the Lower East Sider in me. Not coincidentally, this was also the first poem of mine that said something I really had, in a couple of senses, to say.

Serendipity alert: Just this morning, in reading the *Paris Review* interview of the poet J. D. McClatchy, I encountered this: "It's not that I tried deliberately to disown or disfigure [James Merrill's] influence, but after a while I became less interested in his mannerisms (or so they seemed in *my* hands) and more interested in my subject. Or, less interested in what I was doing, more interested in what I was saying."

The Chance to Choose a Subject

Before I wanted to write poems, I wanted to write music—a calling for which I had, talent excepted, all the necessary equipment. In the years since, I've asked myself more than once if I wouldn't rather have composed, had I been able to, than written poetry. An answer that sometimes comes to mind takes the form of another question: Wouldn't anyone? (Wagner looked forward every morning to sitting down at what he called "the incredible loom.") But sometimes I'm fine with being a poet rather than a composer. On a good day, I can even feel lucky that this is how things turned out. If there's a main reason why, it's because writing a poem gives me the chance to choose a subject.

Like many poets (though by no means all), I have a list of prospective subjects. Which one should I take up next? Sometimes I'll choose the most recently added one, this being the one most freshly charged with discovery. Or I might choose a subject that differs markedly from the last one I chose, the driver here being not discovery but variety. On rare occasions, I'll choose a subject not because it's different from the last one I chose but because it's different from all the subjects I've ever chosen. The motivation here feels larger than variety; feels more like what might be called growth. (Yeats offers a look inside such a development in "The Circus Animals' Desertion," in which he writes of his need to find a theme not among the "masterful images" of his prior work—"Those stilted boys, that burnished chariot, / Lion and woman and the Lord knows what"—but in the source of those images, "the foul rag and bone shop of the heart.")

And then there are times when I choose, from my list of potential subjects, the best one. *Best* can mean, in this as in most contexts, any number of things. I'm thinking here of *best* as in "of greatest moment." Poetry being a human enterprise, the best subject on my list would be the one likeliest to mean the most to the most people. To choose a subject on this basis is to find one's choice expanding beyond purely aesthetic considerations into a consideration of life.

The opportunity to engage with life in choosing a poem's subject is the main reason I sometimes feel fine—maybe even better than fine—about writing poetry instead of music. Choosing a subject in light of life calls upon every faculty we have: intellectual, moral, spiritual, and, yes, aesthetic, to the extent, not always paramount these days, that we want our subjects to underwrite poems whose virtues include beauty. This call for all we have, that we might offer all we can—to what summons would one rather respond?

Which leaves my old feeling of being called to composition . . . where? I remember being shocked to hear myself say, in speaking with a music-loving literary critic, that I thought music was "thin soup" compared to poetry. What I meant was that the matter of poetry—life, language, and the outer and inner worlds these inhabit—was richer, thicker, than the tones and interrelations thereof that constitute music. My interlocutor was content to let the look on her face bespeak her discomfort with this view, but it's easy to imagine the terms in which she might have objected to it: that the "grain" of music is finer than that of poetry (she might have adduced Mendelssohn's assertion that the meanings of music are not too vague but too precise for words); that, considerations of "thickness" or "thinness" to the side, music affords access to emotional depths otherwise un-plumbable.

I wouldn't want to dispute these objections outright—not least because part of me participates in them so wholly—but I don't find them quite conclusive either. I was taught music theory in college by a professor who understood music as deeply as anyone I've ever known. He'd studied viola (that very voice of depth) and composition at one of the major conservatories. In a pensive mood one day, he told me that as indebted as he was to those studies as a person and an artist, he regretted their leaving him without the broader knowledge that a full liberal arts education would have provided. To go by this admirable man's feeling of inadequacy in this regard, his lifelong immersion in music might have especially equipped him to understand, and even sympathize with, a view of music as being "thinner" than poetry. (Perhaps music and poetry can be seen, to borrow a concept from mathematics, as "different orders of infinity," with poetry being the larger, as the infinity of "real numbers" is larger, in being more densely populated, than the infinity of integers.)

Someone once told the great choreographer Mark Morris that he seemed more passionate about music than dance. Morris's response? "Music is more interesting than dance." (After all, he went on, "there are only so many things a dancer can do.") I don't see how my own love of music could be greater than it is, and yet—and if I were a practicing composer instead of a failed one, this might not be the case—I can at least imagine myself saying (when Bach isn't listening) that poetry is more interesting than music.

The Chance to Ponder a Subject
When I was struggling to find my poetic "voice," I was writing very few poems. But that didn't mean I wasn't coming up with ideas for poems.

They circled overhead like planes in a landing pattern, waiting for me to talk them down when I felt ready to. And I knew which one I was going to talk down first.

As a little kid, I'd come into a certain comprehension of death. After all, didn't I already know how it felt to be dead? Hadn't I already been nonexistent? I remember how at night, in bed, I'd try to talk myself into a reexperiencing of this state. "Think of how you felt before you were born," I'd say. "Before George Washington was born. Before *Columbus* was born. . . ." And suddenly I'd be seized with the realization that I was going to be nothing again, and this time forever. In "The Old Fools," Larkin limns this likeness of postexistence to preexistence with his usual, unusual directness where death is concerned:

> It's only oblivion, true:
> We had it before, but then it was going to end,
> And was all the time merging with a unique endeavour
> To bring to bloom the million-petalled flower
> Of being here. Next time you can't pretend
> There'll be anything else.

On those childhood nights, I'd pound the wall beside my bed in a rage at the unappealability of this permanent return to oblivion.

When, twenty-odd years later, I was ready to start applying my newly found poetic voice to my backlog of subjects, the subject I felt I had to tackle first was my dread of death. The others could wait—would have to wait—until I'd given this dread expression.

So I set to work on my "feeling death" poem, as I thought of it—and found myself failing to get very far. The problem wasn't that I couldn't articulate this feeling but that I felt insufficiently authentic in doing so. It was as though I'd, if not outgrown my dread of death, at least grown somewhat out of it. As the pain of a tooth extraction is, if not eliminated, at least dulled by laughing gas, so my dread of death, while still there, didn't hurt as much. (Or to say this differently and perhaps more precisely, I couldn't take the pain as seriously.)

Did this lessening of death dread spell the end of my "feeling death" poem? If so, so be it: I had other subjects waiting to be taken up. . . . Though not so fast. If I'd to some extent outgrown my dread of death, might there be some value in writing about the outgrowing? (A similarly "meta" tack is taken by Yeats toward his struggle, mentioned earlier, to find a subject for "The Circus Animals' Desertion." Having "sought a theme and sought for it in vain," he makes the search itself his theme.) As things turned out, a poem about outgrowing one's dread of death was a poem I could write:

DELIVERANCE

When I think about how
We deal with our mortality
I think about a sense in which it's like we
Deal with an injury.

About how, on first
Comprehending the ultimate
Hurt, we harrow it more nights than not:
This at the behest of that

Cave-old, even
Ocean-old imperative
To reckon at its maximally grave
Any injury we have.

How, years having passed,
We find ourselves assessing it
Far less frequently, and more by rote
Than necessity: our purpose not

To sound the wound so much as
To remind ourselves it's still there.
How one day we're suddenly aware
Of its no longer being there.

I seem to recall someone—Emerson?—saying that writing a poem is a lever that can lift a person to a higher plane of life. And damned if I didn't feel, upon completing this poem, that I'd in fact been so lifted. In the intervening years, I've refined this feeling. It now seems clear that the elevation in question had occurred before I'd even begun the poem, that writing the poem "merely" made me aware of a change I'd already undergone in growing up a little. What also seems clear is that I came to this awareness not during my execution of the poem but during my pondering, prior to execution, of its subject.

Here endeth this little parable—and true story—of what pondering a subject can do for a poet. The case in question was admittedly extreme: such pondering doesn't always abet elevation. But it often abets understanding. I said in the last section that in choosing a subject, a poet engages with life. I've tried to show in this section that in pondering a subject, a poet examines life. It was Socrates, Google tells me, who said that the unexamined life is not worth living. Pondering a subject is a practicum in the examination of life.

The Chance to Treat a Subject

We looked earlier at what the treatment of a subject can do for a poem. It can also do something for a poet.

I've mentioned some of the decisions such treatment can entail: Should the poem show its subject or tell about it? Should the poem digress from its subject? How should the poem's versification (if it has any) relate (if at all) to its subject? Might a poem's subject benefit from being packaged in a "special" form like an echo poem? A shaped poem? A nursery rhyme? Might an elusive subject call for the deployment of an extraordinary "net" of language (Thomas Wyatt: "Since in a net I seek to hold the wind") like the web of verbs with which Dickinson tries to ensnare her "diviner thing"?

Something I haven't mentioned with regard to decisions of treatment is that grappling with them is one of the most absorbing things a poet can do. Frost, looking back from a vantage of many years on the writing of "Birches," said that the poem had its origins in two ideas he'd struggled to put together: a problem he'd solved so long ago that he'd forgotten where in the poem "the seam" between them was. The two ideas were presumably about birches being bent, transiently and fictively, by a boy's swinging on them; and birches being bent, permanently and actually, by ice storms. What were Frost's options regarding these differing, even contradictory ideas? The simplest move would have been to leave one of them out, probably the one about the ice storms (the swinger-of-birches idea presumably being the poem's raison d'être). Or if the ice storms idea was going to be included, it might have been put first, yielding a poem whose train of thought would have been: "When I see birches bend to the left and right, I know they were bent by ice storms. But I'd like to think some boy's been swinging on them." In the event, of course, Frost decided to start "Birches" with the "boy's been swinging on them" idea, only to abandon it after a mere three lines for the ice storms idea . . . then, after giving those ice storms the full beauty treatment, to pick the swinging-on-birches idea back up, thereby revealing the ice storm passage as a digression, surely one of the great digressions in poetry. (By the way, the lines that return us to the swinger-of-birches fancy—"But as I was going to say when Truth broke in / With all her matter-of-fact about the ice storm"—is about as obvious and wonderfully shameless a "seam" as the English language can manage.)

This account of Frost's self-avowed struggle to combine his "two ideas" is speculative, of course. But there's no reason to doubt that combining them *was* a struggle, one that entailed a strenuous exercise of Frost's capabilities as engineer, artist, and philosopher alike. To call such an exercise absorbing, as I did, is to understate what must have been the fascination of it. (Yeats famously spoke of "the fascination of what's difficult.") What poet wouldn't crave such an experience?

I wish I could be sure this question was rhetorical. To put the ice storm idea first or second (if it's included at all); to couch it, or not, as a digression; if it's couched as a digression, to try to hide the seam between the digression and the poem's principal train of thought or, as Frost does, to be cheekily open about the seam—such questions of treatment can't arise if there isn't a subject to treat. Today's poets of discontinuity have largely opted, as a matter of predilection and/

or principle, to exclude subjects from their work. In doing so, they've denied themselves the fascination—even, when things go especially well, the exhilaration—of a struggle such as Frost's.

SOME THINGS SUBJECTS CAN GIVE POETRY

Humanness

For the last half-century, it's been hard to get through even a semester of college without encountering Noam Chomsky's idea that the human brain is hardwired for language. Chomsky didn't see how an infant can acquire speech so quickly if it isn't born with a factory-installed "language organ." This idea has been challenged over the years by some who posit a mental organ enabling not language but logic (language being seen, on this view, as a special case of logic). But you don't hear anyone denying that speech is enabled by an inborn machinery of *some* sort. It's this neuronal lobe, to so envision it, that receives anything communicated verbally: that was born to, is waiting to, is dying to ingest and digest some words.

Here come some words now. They clearly constitute a poem (one knows one anywhere) but a poem that, in Stephanie Burt's words, "leaps . . . from topic to topic" and "lacks . . . a single story line or motive that defines it"—a poem, that is to say, without a subject. What was its author thinking? Here was an opportunity to engage with a mental engine ready, willing, and stupendously able to empathize with any feeling expressed, to picture anything evoked, to follow the progress of any argument or meditation or story—and our poet has chosen to, may even have gone out of his or her way to, feed this engine none of these things. Why would anyone want to starve such a faculty? What could move a person, even so peculiar person as a poet, to be so withholding?

There are answers to this question, but none of them is very convincing. Someone might say they're writing a subjectless poem in the name of novelty. But subjectlessness, like so many other poetic innovations, had been ventured as far back as the early days of modernism.

Someone might say (as we've seen a couple of poets do) that a subject-less poem offers a revealing simulacrum of our mental waywardness. But this waywardness can be discerned without any special assistance from a poem: all that's required is a modicum of introspection.

Or perhaps special assistance is, if not required, at least useful in this connection. Perhaps a poem without a subject affords an especially good look at the chaos that "really" reigns in our heads. But about that *really:* really? To believe this is to believe that the subconscious mind, the presumed site of this free-for-all of thought, is realer than the conscious one, with its (usually) more orderly thought regime. Only some-one spectacularly lacking in self-awareness would deny the existence of the subconscious mind, but why should that mind be seen as realer than the conscious one? That would be like seeing our cerebellum, or "lizard brain," as realer than our cerebral cortex, the presumed seat of higher cognition. The cerebellum certainly goes much further back in evolutionary terms than the cortex, and its doings no doubt provide a substrate for cortical activity, but that doesn't make the cortex any less existent. Similarly, it's widely believed that the self is constructed from a mélange of more primitive elements. But the fact that something is constructed doesn't make it nonexistent (especially if the construct in question has been responsible for, say, the splitting of the atom or the herding of millions into ovens). So no: even if a poetry without subjects gives us a privileged view of the subconscious mind—a sizable *if*—the subconscious mind is no more real than the conscious one. And it's in the ranged galleries of the conscious mind that the language organ resides, hungry for something substantive to consume.

To deprive this organ of a subject is to show contempt for a faculty that, in its huge powers of construal, goes further than any other to-ward making our kind unique. True, other creatures have shown an ability to understand and even manipulate symbols to which meaning has been assigned. A few may even have displayed a rudimentary ca-pacity for syntax. But as far as we know, our capacity for language so greatly surpasses that of any other species (any other terrestrial one anyway) as to make it, effectively, ours alone. When a poem gives this capacity a subject to chew on, the poem engages with an essential aspect of our humanness; may even be said to be endowed, in this respect, with some humanness itself.

Humanness in the arts isn't to everyone's taste. It hasn't been for quite a while, in fact. When the philosopher José Ortega y Gasset wrote his essay "The Dehumanization of Art" in 1925, he was applauding, not denouncing, what he saw as a central aspect of a new development— abstraction—in painting. But other ponderers of the arts have retained a soft spot for the human. Helen Vendler told me that one of the three things she most wanted a poem to be was "human" (the others being "original" and "imbued with thought"). *Homo sapiens* may be on its way out—or, if the species is more fortunate than most, on its way otherward, to some future incarnation. But as long as anything you'd call people are around, their hearts can be expected to harbor some recognizably human qualities. And even when people are no more, perhaps these qualities will live on in the hearts, or heart equivalents, of the new dispensation, should there be one.

Newness

We looked earlier at how newness in a subject can make for newness in a poem. In doing so, we had Pound's famous "Make it new" sounding in our ears. In advancing this injunction, Pound was speaking not of individual poems but of poetry as a whole. Since *we're* now speaking of poetry as a whole, can subjects make poetry new?

In considering this question, we might start by asking what makes any art new. An answer could do worse than begin with a nod to the Enlightenment. This revolution in thought is commonly associated with a questioning of age-old givens in politics, religion, and the sciences. It's less often associated with a questioning of equally ancient givens in the arts. Yet the freedom of thought that drove painting from representation through cubism to abstraction, that drove music from tonality through "free" atonality to the strict atonality of serialism, that drove poetry from formalism through vers libre into fragmentation and surrealism, the freedom of thought that drove all these innovations in the arts had its origins in the ascendance of Reason.

Taken together, these innovations constitute the seismic, early-twentieth-century event in the arts we now call modernism. Like many quakes, the modernist one had its aftershocks. As the decades passed, a continuing spirit of experimentalism drove the work of the most radical artists to the very limits of order ("*total* serialization," that is, the serializing not only of pitch but of all aspects of music; Sol Lewitt's algorithmically generated art; Oulipo's algorithmically generated writing), of chaos (Iannis Xenakis's "stochastic," or chance, music; Robert Rauschenberg's mash-ups; the more extreme strands of "language" poetry), of the maximal (Karlheinz Stockhausen's *Gruppen;* Jackson Pollock's "all-over" paintings, which made some wonder if *painting* was all over; Marcel Proust's *In Search of Lost Time*), of the minimal (John Cage's "4:33" of silence; Ad Reinhardt's "black paintings"; Gertrude Stein at times), all the way to the blurring, even the erasure, of the boundary between art and nonart by Marcel Duchamp's "Urinal," recorded–noises–as–"musique concrète," "found" poetry . . .

Modernism continues to figure importantly in the arts. But the defining breakthroughs of modernism were unrepeatable. The "emancipation of the dissonance" (Schoenberg's phrase), poetry's "first heave" into free verse (Pound's phrase), the elevation of abstraction to the status of art (not "merely" decoration), the elimination of the distinction between art and nonart—these huge discontinuities could occur only once. (Of course, if we're nuked, baked, or flooded back to the Stone Age, all resets are possible.) In both its unrepeatability and its consequentialness, the modernist event might be compared to the cosmic Big Bang (which actually may *not* be unrepeatable, per recent theories of "cyclical" universes and "multiverses" and the like; a cavil that for purposes of the present discussion is, like the universe itself, neither here nor there).

Another source of newness in the arts might be compared to an aspect of the heavens that's closer to our terrestrial home: the weather. I'm thinking of, say, the advent of jazz, a world-changing music that thundered up from the horrifically caused collision of a musically African "air-mass" with a musically European one. Jazz was born, that is to say, from an interfusing of existing realms, for all that the result was as unprecedented as any artistic development de novo. A comparable interfusion underlies the mix of Western European classical music with a Russian strand in Igor Stravinsky, with a Hungarian strand in Béla Bartók, with an Indian strand in Philip Glass. And we see similar if perhaps more modest mixings all the time in popular music, in which new genres are forever arising from an intermingling of existing ones. A paradigm case is the birth of reggae, in which elements of (Jamaican) ska and (American) rhythm and blues interacted—a process catalyzed by some fairy dust sprinkled on the mix by individuals of genius—to produce a new, distinctive, and lasting category of music: an addition, as the critic R. P. Blackmur said of new poetic idioms, to "the stock of available reality." Nor, of course, does cross-cultural intermingling occur only in music. European painting received, via Picasso, an infusion from Africa. In *Ulysses,* James Joyce adapted a tale whose origins lay not just thousands of miles but thousands of years distant from Dublin. An interest in Latin American and Eastern European poetries helped give rise to the "deep image" poetry of Robert Bly, James Wright, and W. S. Merwin. While it's unlikely, to say the least, that any of these particular interfusings will recur, the swirling, cross-cultural "weather" that gave rise to them is, unlike the unrepeatable "Big Bang" of modernism, an ongoing phenomenon.

Beyond the combinatorics of such weather, the arts can also derive newness from what Frost, in "Tree at My Window," called "inner weather": the ever-changing skyscape of the individual mind. This is where subjects fit into the broader picture of poetic innovation. From the swirl of images, ideas, memories, and feelings within each of us, thoughts will sometimes arise that, to quote a certain Scarecrow, have never been "thunk before." (Merwin's "anniversary of my death" idea is a prime specimen.) Such thoughts are, ipso facto, prospective subjects for poems. Some of the more promising ones are those (like Merwin's idea) that cause us to slap our foreheads and say, "Why didn't *I* think of that?" Dickinson went so far as to define a poet as one who

> Distills amazing sense
> From ordinary Meanings—
> And Attar so immense

From the familiar species
That perished by the Door—
We wonder it was not Ourselves
Arrested it—before—

Subjects born of inner weather are an important source of newness in poetry. They can renovate the art not through one-time leaps in form or technique (the move to free verse, Williams's triplet stanzas, e. e. cummings's typographical fantasias) but through a continual generation of fresh substance (as suggested by Frost's evocation, in praising E. A. Robinson's work, of an "old-fashioned way to be new"). Fresh subjects offer potential relief from the feeling of belatedness that commonly afflicts the arts and artists in these postmodern times. It can seem as if all the big breakthroughs have already been made, as if the radical experimenters of the last century pushed every art to its logical limits (which in fact they did). So where is an aspiring innovator to go from here? An answer suggested by the cultural *and* personal weathers of the arts would be—not to "go" anywhere: to adopt, rather, in recognition of any weather's unending generativeness, a conception of the arts as limitless within.

A Place for the World

As a thought experiment, imagine if all poetry had always been subjectless. Think of the many species of poetry—most of them, in fact—that would never have arisen. To name a few in fairly recent memory, the British "pylon poetry" of the 1930s (with its power lines and locomotives), "confessional" poetry, and the poetry that protested the Vietnam War would all have been impossible in a subjectless poetic realm. How can a poem be about an "aeroplane," an affair, or a massacre if it isn't about anything? Pondering this question may lead to a realization so obvious it's easy to overlook: subjects admit the world to poetry.

It would be hard to argue, though a visionary might try, that poetry isn't the better for subjects' hospitality in this regard. Letting the world in can benefit poetry in several major ways. To begin with the most straightforward, it can make poetry more interesting. Why should the

lore of people, places, professions, war, wildlife, faith, and physics en-
rich and enliven only prose? One can get as vivid a sense of statecraft,
say, from Shakespeare as from Machiavelli. (Besides, what would life
or poetry be without some pylons in it?)

Admitting the world can also make poetry more powerful. We've
already seen how the world's presence in Herbert's "The Collar" contributes mightily to that poem's impact: how the "large muscle" of the
poem's subject, a fierce resistance to religious stricture, makes a last-
minute submission to that stricture so momentous. If we pull back
from the individual poem to poetry in general, we see a larger-scale
version of such a "power train" everywhere in action. Consider the rise
of confessional poetry. This literary development had its origins in a
societal one: a loosening of mores that admitted intimate, disturbing,
even shocking revelations to public discussion. Poetry was swept up
in this liberalizing current. The work that resulted had its variousness,
but no small portion of it, from the harrowing, wife's-eye view of coitus
in Robert Lowell's "'To Speak of Woe That Is in Marriage'": "'Gored by
the climacteric of his want, / he stalls above me like an elephant'"; to
the ack-ack Sylvia Plath spits at her "Daddy":

I have always been scared of *you,*
With your Luftwaffe, your gobbledygoo.
And your neat mustache
And your Aryan eye, bright blue.
Panzer-man, panzer-man, O You——

to the steely rhetoric, in "Beyond Harm," with which Sharon Olds for-
tifies herself as she recalls *her,* er, difficult father:

        He respected
my spunk—when they had tied me to the chair, that time,
they were tying up someone he respected, and when
he did not speak for weeks I was one of the
beings to whom he was not speaking

—no small portion of such poetry has a power that originates in the larger world (often in the mammoth aspect of the world called family dynamics) and flows into a given poem through the particularized instance of a subject.

A third thing admitting the world can do for poetry is give it a moral dimension. The poetry protesting the Vietnam War is one of many manifestations of a moral impulse in verse. To name a few others, there's ecopoetry, the "poetry of witness"—Carolyn Forché's term for poems, like so many of her own, that testify directly to the most extreme horrors of human existence—and, just recently, an efflorescence of what might be called a "poetry of difference": a poetry giving voice to those who are societally disadvantaged, often grievously, sometimes even fatally, by their gender, race, faith, nationality, ethnicity, sexuality, or disability.

For some people, the cries of the downtrodden are always in earshot. For many of us, however, these cries are considerably less constant a presence. We go about our business largely oblivious to them—only, on occasion, to find them filling our heads. It's as though we become at these times the vessels and vassals of compassion our better selves feel we should always be, even if we presently revert to our otherwise occupied/preoccupied selves.

The occasional accesses in our lives of a moral imperative have a parallel in our dealings with poetry. There we are, ambling along in the poppy fields of poesy, when suddenly, amid the swim of stems and blossoms, a poem of conscience arrests us. Such a poem may shock its way out of the mass. An example from the "poetry of witness"—perhaps the classic example—is Forché's "The Colonel." On a trip to El Salvador, the poet has accepted an invitation to dine at the house of the eponymous officer:

The colonel returned with a sack used to bring groceries
home. He spilled many human ears on the table. They were like
dried peach halves. There is no other way to say this. He took one
of them in his hands, shook it in our faces, dropped it into a water
glass. It came alive there. I am tired of fooling around he said. As

for the rights of anyone, tell your people they can go fuck themselves. He swept the ears to the floor with his arm and held the last
of his wine in the air. Something for your poetry, no? he said. Some
of the ears on the floor caught this scrap of his voice. Some of the
ears on the floor were pressed to the ground.

   May 1978

The power of this account is hardly increased and yet enriched, it
seems to me, by some context Forché provides for the poem in an interview with Bill Moyers: "I don't think the Colonel realized that what
I said about myself was true—I really was just a twenty-seven-year-old
American poet. He got a little intoxicated and angry, and he wanted to
send a message to the Carter administration. He wanted me to go back
to Washington and tell President Carter, 'We've had enough of this
human rights policy,' and his actions were his way of demonstrating
his contempt." (Forché goes on to say that the image of ears pressed to
the ground, which "sometimes people are puzzled" by, is a reference to
the expression "'ear to the ground,' you know the way you can hear a
train coming if you put your ear to the ground?")

   Shock isn't the only tactic available to a poem of moral force. In
Langston Hughes's "Let America Be America Again," it's the quiet irony
of his indictment that makes it so heartbreaking:

Let America be America again.
Let it be the dream it used to be.
Let it be the pioneer on the plain
Seeking a home where he himself is free.

(America never was America to me.)

Let America be the dream the dreamers dreamed—
Let it be that great strong land of love
Where never kings connive nor tyrants scheme
That any man be crushed by one above.

(It never was America to me.)

By shocking us, by moving us, by whatever means a poem of conscience takes possession of us, the dominion it assumes tends to be, while it lasts, absolute. Such a poem may send other kinds of poetry scuttling in shame into the shadows of our regard. But as with most epiphanies, we can bear the intensity of this one only so long: sooner or later (probably sooner), the immense rest of poetry reasserts its claim on our interests and affections. Yet encounters with poems as morally authoritative as "The Colonel" or "Let America be America Again" may leave us, as readers and people, at least a *little* changed.

Until just recently, it seemed as though subjectless poems might be on their way to dominance. In some quarters, they may even have attained it. But as mentioned earlier, poetry without subjects is now giving ground to a socially and politically engaged poetry of difference. It's hard to see how this or any poetry with a moral dimension can do without subjects. That said, a poetry that seeks to go beyond subjects is hardly disappearing. And a good thing it isn't: may there always be a strain in poetry that looks past subjects to the transcendent, the visionary, even the incoherent. But may there always be as well an interrogation of this strain by those who see poetry as less than its largest without a place for subjects.

3

Working with Subjects

"The trouble with you, Robert," a tipsy Wallace Stevens once said to a less (but nonetheless) tipsy Robert Frost, "is that you write about—subjects."

So that's what's wrong with my poems. Oh well, too late to swear off subjects now. In working with them, there are certain approaches I've found especially helpful and haven't seen discussed elsewhere. So I thought I might say a little about them here. In doing so, I've quoted some poems of mine. No claim for them is implied; it just seemed natural, in talking about my dealings with particular subjects, to offer a look at the poems these subjects gave rise to.

FINDING SUBJECTS

Where does a poem's subject come from? Larkin's way of answering this question would be hard to improve on. He was once asked, with reference to his poem "Toads," how he came up with the idea of the toad as a metaphor for nine-to-five work. His response? "Sheer genius."

End of section. Or so it could and maybe should be. Yet there may be at least a little to say about if not finding subjects—it isn't clear we do find subjects, not by searching for them anyway—then about recognizing when subjects find us.

One commonly hears that a poet in need of a subject should wait in receptive stillness for something to strike, like those physicists monitoring giant tanks of liquid boron for a hit from the occasional neutrino. I see nothing wrong with such an aggressively passive approach to subject acquisition, though in my own experience, the odds of being struck by a subject are the same—extremely low—whether I'm sitting in the lotus position or dashing for a bus. (They do go up a little when I'm standing in the shower.)

Given the slim chance of being struck by a subject at all, it's especially unfortunate when you're struck by one without realizing it. There are some subjects, of course, whose potential is impossible to miss. If Merwin didn't sit bolt upright when the "anniversary of my death" idea hit him, there really is no certainty in this world. Most poets will say they've received at least a few such happy visitations. To take a case of my own: once, in the midst of a love I was in, I found myself wishing I believed in God so I would have something suitably huge to thank for such bliss—and thinking that if I couldn't make a poem out of this wish, I should hand in my poetic license. Here's the poem that resulted:

THE BIRTH OF GOD

It happened near Lascaux
Millions of dawns ago.
For dawn it was,
Infusing radiance
And cuing avians
The way it does,

That saw the two of them
(Odds are a her and him,
Though maybe not)
Emerging from the mouth
Of a cave a couple south
Of the one that's got

All that painted fauna
All but snorting on a
Wall. That is
To say, from the mouth of a cave
Unconsecrated save
By the sighs and cries

Of the night just past. The pair
Has borne the bliss they share
Out into the bright.
Where silently they stand
Thanking, hand in hand
Before the light.

Their gratitude is truly
New beneath the duly
Erupting sun.
A gratitude that so
Wants a place to go
It authors one.

Then there are subjects whose potential is anything *but* obvious. Yet something about them whispers in our ear; something in them wants to be gotten at, or to, if only we can bring it out (or reel it in). A wonderful poem with a seemingly unpromising subject is E. A. Robinson's "The Sheaves." The poem is about, for want of a better word, wheat. Yet look at the marvel Robinson makes of wheat and words alike:

Where long the shadows of the wind had rolled,
Green wheat was yielding to the change assigned;
And as by some vast magic undivined
The world was turning slowly into gold.
Like nothing that was ever bought or sold
It waited there, the body and the mind;
And with a mighty meaning of a kind
That tells the more the more it is not told.

So in a land where all days are not fair,
Fair days went on till on another day
A thousand golden sheaves were lying there,
Shining and still, but not for long to stay—
As if a thousand girls with golden hair
Might rise from where they slept and go away.

And then there are times, as I've suggested, when a subject's potential, though evident enough, escapes our notice. In the fall of 1963, our
high school class took a day trip to Princeton University. The trip included attendance at a Princeton student production of a Restoration
play. The play's final curtain took longer than usual to come back up,
and when it did, only one person was standing there: no one in the
cast but an older man in a jacket and tie. He lifted a hand to quiet our
smattering of uncertain applause (was this some kind of "educational"
substitute for a curtain call?) and told us—but I'll let the poem I wrote
about this incident relate the rest of it:

WHERE I WAS

I was in Princeton of all
Places. My ninth grade class
Was enduring a tour of the U: a forgettable
Shepherding from edifice
To edifice—no end of gray
Stone—winding up, though,
With something a little out of the way:
The opportunity to view
A classic three-acter
At the U's own theater.

The play I don't remember much
About: a hoary exercise
In wigs and bodices and such.
The memorable thing was
The curtain call. How the one

Coming out was a grim guy
In tweed and tie. How the lone
Lifting of his palm by
Itself extinguished the applause.
How he had "terrible news"—

But not the news I feared. Not
Where to go (to a room below-
Ground). Not how to get
There. Not what to do
There: sit on the floor, put
Your head down, clasp your hands
Behind your head, you might shut
Your eyes in case the world ends—
None of that. Maybe he
Was finding it decidedly

Hard to get the words out,
But what the words amounted to
Wasn't the worst thing: not
Anything that had to do
With going up in a solar hell,
But rather with the President,
A motorcade, a hospital—
With how the evident extent
Of anybody's sudden death
Was elsewhere and over with.

In the years following this experience, I must have told the story of it to
dozens of people. Yet what seems obvious now—that a poem might be
made of this story—never occurred to me. Until, maybe twenty years
on, it did—in part, I suspect, because I'd begun making poems out of
things that, like this story, I might really say to people, poetry to the side.

I've related how I "found my voice" in trying for the first time to
write such a poem. But a voice wasn't the only thing I garnered from
this attempt; I also gained access to a new realm of subject matter. The

idea of a subject as "something to say" can help explain this development. Because what sorts of things *do* we say—in real life, I mean? The
mouth's default position is shut; what might move us to open it? The
most fundamental spur to speech may be the impulse to greet. Frost
has an underappreciated little poem that bears on this impulse, not to
say obligation, called "A Time to Talk":

> When a friend calls to me from the road
> And slows his horse to a meaning walk,
> I don't stand still and look around
> On all the hills I haven't hoed,
> And shout from where I am, What is it?
> No, not as there is a time to talk.
> I thrust my hoe in the mellow ground,
> Blade-end up and five feet tall,
> And plod: I go up to the stone wall
> For a friendly visit.

(A "meaning walk": if *that* brilliant locution doesn't evoke a whole
under-universe of social codes.) And once we've opened a line to
someone, what sorts of communications do we put on it? A question,
a report, an assertion, a request, a proposal. . . . Most of this content
will be utilitarian, the mundane stuff that helps us get through the day.
But sometimes we're moved to speak by an impulse to share: to impart
something so good—so interesting, so funny, so moving, so illuminating, even, if we're feeling prophetic, so revelatory—that keeping it to
ourselves is more than we can bear. (Frost, in an appearance at Sarah
Lawrence College: "A think. And the excitement you get out of *having*
a think. That you want to pass on to other people.") Such share-worthy
material can be fresh and fertile soil for subjects.

This suggestion needs some qualifying. Yes, a subject can be something you'd really say to someone—but about that someone, it's best
to imagine him or her as not knowing you from a hole in the wall. If
what you're saying would interest the proverbial "stranger on a train,"
it has at least a fighting chance of interesting that stranger writ large,

the reader. And when I suggest using something you really have to say as a subject, I'm including things you might nonetheless be hesitant to say. My hesitation to say the following lasted many years:

STANDING

I've never been in a fight;
Not the real kind
Where you want to hurt a guy
You might get damaged by:
A fact that one could find
A little peculiar, right?

If I could pull some strings
And have myself remade
As someone with the guts . . .
Of all the sorry thoughts
A thinker's ever had.
Among the primal things

A god could not undo
Is a wont to run away.
Were a son of mine to come
Under a bully's thumb,
I'd know the words to say,
But lack the standing to.

Also: while a subject *can* be something you'd say in real life, it doesn't have to be. I make so self-evident a point only because, for a time, it wasn't evident to me. When I first began basing poems on things I might really say, I was so excited by the possibilities of this approach—not least by the realization that such non-"poetic" material was even eligible for poetry—that I found myself putting my prospective subjects to an "imagine myself really saying this" test. (To make this test sufficiently stringent, I imagined myself speaking to a guy in the office where I worked—no fan of poetry as far as I knew but a savvy son of a gun—named Spike.) This procedure served me well enough until I hit on the idea for my "Birth of God" poem. I could have treated this idea "straight"—could have told in direct, or at least direct-ish, terms how I wished I believed in God so I could thank something suitably huge for my being in love—but found the idea morphing into the poem's mini-tale of what "happened in Lascaux"; into something, that is, that I couldn't imagine myself saying in real life to anyone (least of all to Spike). This development left me with a binary choice: either accept that my subjects needn't always pass the "imagine myself saying this" test or abandon my poem-in-prospect about the birth of God. Guess which way I went?

In the years since, I've come to see this choice as a false one. I now *can* imagine telling a stranger what happened in Lascaux: maybe not a stranger on a train but a stranger aboard the conveyance called a poem. In his extraordinary treatise *The Poem,* the poet and critic Don Paterson has some interesting and persuasive things to say about what he calls the "contract" between poem and reader. To encapsulate his comments: lodged as a poem usually is within constraints of space (the white borders surrounding it) and time (a promise, in most cases, to be reasonably brief), it will compensate for and/or leverage these constraints by speaking with economy, originality, and one or more aspects of patterning (meter, rhyme, stanza . . .). These traits leave the reader "with a piece of text often identifiable as a poem by its brazen lack of self-explanation, its original phrasemaking and its ostentatiously 'poem-like' shape. Were we to read this text as a 'normal' piece of prose, or within the framework of conversational speech, we would likely identify these features as respectively discontinuous, alien and artificial. The contract of poetry, however, is that we agree to see none of these things, but instead a wholly natural language-game in which poet and reader collude." (Isn't there a comparable "collusion" between fiction writer and reader? If we're okay with a piece of prose that opens with something as conversationally preposterous as "Once upon a time"—not to say "Stately, plump Buck Mulligan"—it's because we know we're listening to "a story" and make allowances for that odd sort of voice we recognize as the storytelling one.) When I hold Paterson's set of agreed-upon poetic traits up against my "Birth of God" poem, I'm tempted to add an optional additional one: fancy. A prose fable version of what happened in Lascaux is certainly imaginable, but poetry is another natural habitat for the contrafactual.

This last point was brought home to me with particular force by a poem I undertook shortly after I'd written "The Birth of God." As I was watching a nature documentary about the Pacific salmon, I found myself imagining a specimen so enchanted with the wonders of the sea that it doesn't want to go back to—not to mention leap exhaustingly back up—the river of its birth. The poem that resulted is spoken *by* this aberrant salmon (which admittedly sounds in spots as though it's been watching some nature documentaries itself).

A SALMON SPEAKS OF THE SEA

You approach it
with an image of it
but nothing prepares you for it.

Shot with sun in its upper reaches,
a bankless realm dims in descent,
gradually devolving toward a blackness
one fins through life
trying not to think about.

Yet up from that nethernight
jut those peaks and ridges
that provide so much of the grandeur here.
Much of the interest, too,
their faces being
very carnivals of incident.
Especially compelling
are those dramas it's healthier
to witness than to live.
How some of them stay with me!
Like that silverlittle's despondent swim

right down the throat of an anemone:
as though loveloss
had crushed it past caring.
Never more finally
has a clutch of red wormicles
closed over its hole.

And yet...
the giant fans,
slow-asway
in the waterwind...
the manta ray,
its glide a thing
of a ripple of wing...
the jellyfish,
a parachette
comprised of light...
in singing these sublimities,
I ask the several
to stand for the innumerable.

Such richesse!
The river was nice
but never like this.
I have no intention
of ever getting over it.

Here was something I couldn't begin to imagine myself saying in real
life (assuming human and piscine life to be different things). That set-
tled it: my recently adopted stance on subjects—an insistence that
they be things I really had, forget poetry, to say—had given way to a
realization that at least some of my subjects might be suitable *only* for
poems. If the notion of a subject as "something to say" had enlarged
my sense of the poetic, the poetic had returned the favor by enlarging
my sense of what I had to say.

As I look back on this admitting of the poetic to my poetry, what stands out to me is its absurdity. How could I not have welcomed the poetic to my poems from the beginning? Actually I had—until I hit on my "things I might really say" notion. As can happen with any new idea, this one carried me away: swept me so far off the continent of poetry that I lost sight of its shore. But even after I'd regained enough of my bearings to start dog-paddling back, I found that my immersion in the main of saying had helped make me the poet I've been, in the main, ever since.

IMPROVING SUBJECTS

However it got there—by being found, recognized, or airdropped in—a prospective subject has made it into your hands. As you prepare to execute on this subject, your idea of it may be tentative, vague, even inchoate. (Don Paterson says his poems begin with a "hunch.") A number of poets hold that a poem's subject comes into focus only in the course of the poem's being written. Cecil Day-Lewis puts it this way: "I do not sit down at my desk to put into verse something that is already clear in my mind. If it were clear in my mind, I should have no incentive or need to write about it. We do not write in order to be understood; we write in order to understand." Richard Hugo concurs (enlisting W. H. Auden and, indirectly, E. M. Forster as wingmen): "One mark of a beginner is his impulse to push language around to make it accommodate what he has already conceived to be the truth. [Tell this to Yeats, who sought to "beat against the wall / Till Truth obeyed his call."] Even Auden, clever enough at times to make music conform to truth, was fond of quoting the woman in the Forster novel who said something like, 'How do I know what I think until I see what I've said.'" Paterson's version of this view is admirably succinct. Poets "generally write to find out *what* they think, not to 'commit a thought to poetry.'" These eminent poets are all saying that one takes a "blurry" subject in hand and commences execution, in the course of which the subject comes into focus.

This is certainly how things sometimes go. But sometimes a prospective subject is already clear: all that remains is to develop it into a poem that does justice to it. (Like every poet, I've learned the hard way how huge this "all" can be.) My day trip to Princeton was a subject of this already-clear kind. Once I recognized its potential *as* a subject, I knew that if I recounted the experience pretty much as it happened, I'd probably get at least a passable poem out of it.

This doesn't mean a clear subject can't undergo a significant change in the course of a poem's being written. But since the subject is already clear, the change won't be one of clarification. I used to be involved with a woman a little taller than me. I noticed that when I was standing next to her, I'd stand straighter than usual in hopes of matching her height. It occurred to me that if I were ever involved with someone a lot taller than me, there'd be no point in even trying to match her height (I almost said "match her stature"). Here was a *perfectly* clear subject, one whose development into a poem I duly commenced. Things were going well, it seemed—until, in the poem's last couple of lines, it felt like things were going better still.

AT EASE

It's only a theory, and only a theory's what
It'll probably remain, but were I ever
To get involved with somebody a *lot*
Taller than me, her being so would deliver
The two of us from the tension that attends
On the woman's being only a little taller.
No point in my attempting to make amends
For so great a differential (after all, her
Chin is at the level of my pate)
By some technique—say, straightening up—or other;
A futile effort she'd reciprocate
By slouching? Wearing flats? Why even bother?
What is there for a pair so disparate
In something but to be at ease with it?

I'd had the good fortune—at least I think it was good—to find, in a light subject, a potential to be weightier. It wasn't that a vague subject had been clarified, as in the process described by Day-Lewis, Hugo, and Paterson. An already-clear subject, rather, had become not clearer than it had been but more than it had been.

It's true that this had occurred, as per Day-Lewis, Hugo, and Paterson, during the poem's execution. But sometimes a subject, clear or otherwise, undergoes a change prior to execution. A case in point was the subject of my "Birth of God" poem. The morphing of this subject from its "straight" form—a wish that I had a God to thank for a love I was in—into a happening in Lascaux took place before I ever picked up a pen (or even reached for one). All I can add about this morphing is that it happened in a flash.

A pre-execution alteration of a subject can also happen more gradually (and less transformatively). A while back I saw an exhibition of Edward Hopper's drawings. These included preparatory sketches for his paintings. Having chosen, from the dizzying bounty of the visible, a subject, Hopper takes sketchpad and pencil in hand and limns this subject's essentials: its objects, their placement, their orientation. At the same time, he plays with these essentials, moving that house a little to the left, eliminating or adding a streetlight, lowering or raising the angle of view. . . . To follow along with these adjustments is to feel that they're motivated not only by considerations of design—symmetry, balance, proportion—but also by a desire on Hopper's part to draw out from his subject what drew him to it in the first place: its interest or import or truth. (Hopper, on his *Nighthawks:* "I simplified the scene a great deal and made the restaurant bigger [than the one I used as a model]. Unconsciously, probably, I was painting the loneliness of a large city.")

It's worth reiterating that this adjusting of a subject is done before Hopper picks up his brushes. A good thing, too, because such adjusting presumably becomes harder once painting proper is underway. For all the talk of an artist's freedom in the course of execution, there's an important sense in which an artist is even freer prior to execution. And not just a visual artist. Before beginning a novel, Henry James

would modify its originating "germ"—an anecdote overheard at a din-
ner party, say—in order to bring out its dramatic and moral potential.
James was never at greater liberty to alter a novel's essentials than
during these preliminary tinkerings. Something similar applies to poetry. Ted Hughes, for one, seems to have recognized this. "Whatever
we work at, in the way of imaginative creation," he says, our selection
of subject matter is "the last point, almost, at which our choice can still
operate." That *almost* suggests the creative space I'm speaking of: one
in which the poet, having chosen his or her subject, is free to interro-
gate, meditate, and reshape it prior to execution.

Here's where I should adduce some canonical poets' accounts, à la
James's, of such preliminary modification of a subject. And I would if
I could find any. Eminent poets seem more than happy to talk about
their modification, mid-execution, of a poem (sometimes incorporat-
ing draft material in the discussion) but not about their modification,
pre-execution, of a poem's subject. Surely some of them sometimes
partake of the latter. So why no accounts of their doing so? Might
they be enchanted to distraction by the "magical" inadvertency of a
subject's *midstream* shiftings? Whatever the reason for the dearth of
such testimony, I'm reduced to offering some from a poet the canon
has inexplicably overlooked.

I used to live in a seventh-story apartment in Manhattan whose
kitchen window gave on Riverside Park and the Hudson River beyond.
But this prospect had its limitations. I could see the river's grandeur
only in winter, when the intervening trees in the park were bleakly
bare. In the summer, the trees were in glorious leaf—thereby block-
ing my view of the river. I wrote to a friend that this impossibility of
having it all, view-wise, was "an emblem of our plight." Over the years,
I'd occasionally think about doing this predicament up as a poem, but
my shoulders would slump at the anticipated tedium of laying out the
situation's physical setup—the apartment, its location and elevation,
its view—and so I never attempted the piece. Then, not long ago, I
found myself again pondering the poem's possibilities and recalling
the phrase *emblem of our plight.* It occurred to me that the poem could
be cast as, well, emblematic: that laying out the physical setup needn't

be burdensome because I didn't *have* to lay it out; I could leave it out.
Suddenly the poem seemed worth a try.

ISN'T THAT THE WAY

A river's winter-silver
Discerned through screening trees
Takes on a certain sorrow
From the barrenness of these;

Of these whose summer glory
Can seem a little sad,
There being not a glimmer
Of river to be had.

Another such case: In being visited for the umpteenth time by the
commonplace thought that a novelist makes a point not by asserting
it but by making a story of it, I found this thought leading to a further
one: that God, to the extent that I understood a believer's view of Him,
also makes His points narratively. He does this, however, by a narrative means peculiarly His own: not by telling a story but by making
the events in a story actually take place. In pondering this thought,
I found Christ working his way into it as someone who sometimes
makes a point by asserting it ("The meek shall inherit the earth") but
at other times makes a point, like the novelist and God, by means of a
story (in Christ's case, a parable). Voilà: a possible subject for a poem.
But when, having decided to execute on this subject, I held it up for
inspection, it seemed too complicated; seemed as though it had too
many moving parts. What, I wondered, if I were to remove the novelist from it? Wouldn't what remained—an analogy between God and
Christ—be stronger and more focused for the simplification? Mulling
this possibility led to one thought more: that to a Christian, all of
God's stories feed tributary-like into the story of . . . Christ, whose
Crucifixion is seen as the culmination of history. Whereupon God,
Christ, and "story" had linked up in a kind of conceptual Möbius strip
that *did* seem feasible as a poem.

HIS FATHER'S SON

When rather than a verity
He'd offer up a parable,
Christ was being his Father's son,
His Father being another one
For a story (the author, if you will,
Of all that came to Calvary).

In the previous two examples, a subject was improved through simplification. But this isn't always the case. When I was a little kid, I fantasized that my every waking moment was being broadcast to beings on another world who were curious about ours. In due course, this fantasy made it onto a list I keep of prospective subjects—where it sat for decades. Because wasn't such fantasizing utterly unremarkable (the possible oddness of this version of it notwithstanding)? Wasn't it just another case of an infantile megalomania whose presence in one more tyke was neither noteworthy nor illuminating?

A dud of a subject, then . . . until it occurred to me that this fantasy in some ways prefigured my impulse to write. The fantasy alone? Hardly worth a poem. Nor, for that matter, was my impulse to write, which surely didn't differ from that of many other writers. But the fantasy as the impulse in embryo? With the overlaying of a second aspect on its initial one, a stillborn subject had suddenly become viable.

PRESCIENCE

Of course there were dreams of super powers
(Where cars and even trucks were hurled)
But also an odder one: that I
(Who else?) had been selected by
Some beings on another world
To offer them a look at ours

By feeding their collective sight
With everything that met my eyes.

An infantile fantasy. . . .
Which may be why it's taken me
Most of a life to recognize
The prescience of it: how, despite

Its dating from so early on,
Its adumbration of the pair
Of differing yet intertwined
Desires by which I've been defined—
A yen to star, a rage to share—
Could hardly have been improved upon.

If a flawed subject can sometimes be "fixed," a subject that seems perfectly fine can prove irremediably flawed. I used to teach a college music appreciation course. Music being first of all something heard, I began the course by asking the students to write an account of a moment when what they were hearing—it didn't have to be music— seemed central. Little did I suspect the degree to which some of them would open up in response. One of them offered a childhood memory of hearing, through her bedroom wall, her parents arguing. Another wrote of hearing a pop song that made him recognize a beloved as the one he shouldn't have walked away from. (In the event, they got back together; maybe if the workman in Hardy's "In the Moonlight" had had that song on his playlist. . . .) A third had done a stint in the army, during which he'd been deployed to a combat zone. He wrote of the cries of a platoon mate whose intestines were spilling out. . . .

This music class assignment made it onto my subjects list a long time ago. Every time I see it there, I feel an urge to take it up—and then the urge subsides. My problem with this subject, to the extent that I can determine it, is that any poem it might give rise to would be too pat in its sentiments. I have a similar but even stronger reaction to another subject that's been on my list forever. In walking along a suburban street, I saw dozens of sheets of typewritten paper blowing about. I picked a couple up: pages from a filing for divorce. You can bet *that* occurrence made it onto my subjects list. But when I see this subject there, I'm not even tempted to tackle it, so cringe-makingly obvious would be the symbolism in any poem I might make of it. I'm reminded of some words of Don Paterson's: "If you 'get a good idea for a poem,' I'd suggest you run a mile, as this generally isn't the way poems make themselves known." Advice worth attending to—though it's also worth noting the little out Paterson gives himself with that *generally.* I'm glad I didn't run from the good ideas, as I took them to be, for my poems about those lovers in Lascaux, that day trip to Princeton, that sea-smitten salmon. The eminent musicologist Donald Grout used to say, regarding the "rules" of composition, that they're only what composers do "as a rule."

REALIZING SUBJECTS

So you've hammered a subject into as good a shape as you can. Now to realize that subject. By *realize,* I mean fulfill the subject's potential both to become something and to do something: to become a poem and to imbue that poem with interest or import or truth.

Not all subjects are equally endowed with potential. Consider Robinson's earlier-cited "The Sheaves." In and of itself, this poem's subject—wheat—offers it only so much (not much). The magic of "The Sheaves" derives from the brilliancies of thought and phrasing and versification and imagination that Robinson lavishes on his subject (culminating in his incomparable comparison of a thousand sheaves to "a thousand girls with golden hair"). Conversely, sometimes a subject offers a poem a great deal. The subject of Frost's "Neither Out Far nor In Deep," for instance—the ever-seaward gazing of "the people along the shore"—is pre-charged with import. I'm not saying that the poem could have done without the wonderful touches that Frost, like Robinson, applies to his subject. I've acknowledged that "Neither Out Far" wouldn't be nearly the marvel it is without its reflected gull and ship that keeps raising its hull. But a poem with a subject as powerfully suggestive as this one's has something far from negligible going for it even before the application of any local strokes. When Don Paterson says that "the 'idea' alone has no poetic value," it seems to me that he goes too far. I'd suggest, rather, that the "idea" (that is, the subject) of a poem can vary in value, from the minimal value of a subject like that of "The Sheaves" to the considerable value of a subject like that of "Neither Out Far," with the value of a subject like that of, say, Tennyson's "The Eagle" somewhere in between. (Henry James, in his preface to *The Ambassadors:* "There are degrees of merit in subjects.") As these examples makes clear, in any of these cases the result can be a masterpiece.

The process by which a subject's potential is realized is called writing. And something I've found especially helpful in writing is planning. Planning via outlining is generally viewed as a best practice in the writing of even short pieces of expository prose. (The *New York Times's* David Brooks says he outlines his newspaper columns, not to mention his books.) Though outlining is hardly universal among writers of fiction—Faulkner said all he had in mind when he began writing *The Sound and the Fury* was an image of a girl sitting on a tree branch with her muddy underwear showing—it has its proponents among this contingent as well. Giants like Henry James and Toni Morrison (whose outlining is shown in an *American Masters* documentary) to the side, P. G. Wodehouse said he wouldn't dream of trying to construct the Rube Goldberg devices known as his novels without a "scenario" in hand. (There's a sizable body of commercial software designed to facilitate the outlining of fiction specifically.)

Poets, on the other hand, typically disdain planning—perhaps because, apostles of spontaneity that they tend to be, they're loath to associate their creative flights with anything as pedestrian as a plan. God forbid they should be caught at their writing desks with a slide rule as well as a pen. (Note to readers of the future: see Wikipedia to learn what a slide rule was, or a pen for that matter.) Poets commonly speak of planning as injurious, even fatal, to a poem.

It's with a mix of feelings then—shame, trepidation, and foolishness might be mentioned—that I confess to having planned not a few poems of my own. I might add, by way of bucking myself up, that I'm not sure my having done so is as shameful as all that. Should planning really be limited to prose in the literary sphere? Some poems are as unimaginable without planning as *The Portrait of a Lady*. I can't prove

Dante drew up a blueprint for the *Commedia,* but you'd have a hard time convincing me he didn't.

"But that's the *Commedia,*" a poet might object. "Surely a lyric poem doesn't require a blueprint." So far, so inarguable. But when poets push this point further and say that a lyric shouldn't, even can't, be planned . . .

Yeats would sometimes write a prose "sketch" of a poem before launching into execution. One such sketch is for the following poem (his penultimate one), "Cuchulain Comforted." (Cuchulain was a mythic Irish warrior-hero.)

> A man that had six mortal wounds, a man
> Violent and famous, strode among the dead;
> Eyes stared out of the branches and were gone.
>
> Then certain Shrouds that muttered head to head
> Came and were gone. He leant upon a tree
> As though to meditate on wounds and blood.
>
> A Shroud that seemed to have authority
> Among those bird-like things came, and let fall
> A bundle of linen. Shrouds by two and three
>
> Came creeping up because the man was still
> And thereupon that linen-carrier said:
> 'Your life can grow much sweeter if you will
>
> 'Obey our ancient rule and make a shroud:
> Mainly because of what we only know
> The rattle of those arms makes us afraid.
>
> 'We thread the needles' eyes, and all we do
> All must together do.' That done, the man
> Took up the nearest and began to sew.
>
> 'Now must we sing and sing the best we can,
> But first you must be told our character:
> Convicted cowards all, by kindred slain

'Or driven from home and left to die in fear.'
They sang, but had nor human tunes nor words,
Though all was done in common as before;

They had changed their throats and had the throats of birds.

In *Our Secret Discipline,* a pioneering study of the relation between form and content in Yeats, Helen Vendler helpfully explicates this mysterious poem (the casting of whose stanzas in Dante's terza rima—the only use of this form in all of Yeats's work—carries, as Vendler notes, an extra significance given the poem's underworld setting): "Cuchulain, who has always lived by the code of the warrior, is instructed to discard his arms, take up a length of linen, and sew a shroud as his new companions do. It is only after he obeys and begins to sew that the Shrouds tell him the nature of their character and the experience he can expect to undergo with them in this phase: they are "'Convicted cowards all, by kindred slain' // 'Or driven from home and left to die in fear.'" After this revelation the Shrouds begin to sing, their voices transmuted to birdsong." Vendler has already prepared her reference to "this phase": "In Yeats's purgatorial afterlife myth, enunciated in *A Vision,* one phase ('the Shiftings') requires that the dead person experience the opposite of the emotional and moral code he had adopted during his life on earth, in order (as is said in 'The Man and Echo') to 'complete his partial mind.' Cuchulain, who has always lived by the code of the warrior, is instructed to discard his arms, take up a length of linen, and sew a shroud as his new companions do."

Here's Yeats's prose sketch for the poem:

A shade recently arrived went through a valley in the Country of the Dead; he had six mortal wounds, but he had been a tall, strong, handsome man. Other shades looked at him from the trees. Sometimes they went near to him and then went away quickly. At last he sat down, he seemed very tired. Gradually the shades gathered round him, and one of them who seemed to have some authority among the others laid a parcel of linen at his feet. One of the others said: "I am not so afraid of him now that he is sitting still. It was the way his arms rattled." Then another shade said: "You would be much more comfortable if you would make a shroud and wear it instead of the arms. We have brought you some linen. If you make it yourself you will be much happier, but of course we will thread the needles, so that when we have laid them at your feet you will take whichever you like the best." The man with the six wounds saw that nobody had ever threaded needles so swiftly and so smoothly. He took the threaded needles and began to sew, and one of the shades said: "We will sing to you while you sew, but you will like to know who we are. We are the people who ran away from the battles. Some of us have been put to death as cowards, but others have hidden, and some even died without people knowing they were cowards." Then they began to sing, and they did not sing like men and women, but like linnets that had been stood on a perch and taught by a good singing master.

This sketch isn't a draft of the poem, not even a "prose draft," assuming such a thing wouldn't be a contradiction in terms. Yeats, rather, is taking his poem-in-prospect for a kind of conceptual test drive prior to execution per se. His intent, presumably, is to check the contemplated poem for feasibility and potential effectiveness as well as to create a kind of roadmap for it. Is this sketch an instance of planning? I wouldn't insist on the term, but I would say that the sketch is preparatory and, as such, sits uncomfortably within a model of poetic composition that has spontaneity at its heart. Knowing that Yeats—Yeats!—would sometimes sketch a poem makes me rest more easily with my own pre-execution preparations.

An additional point about Yeats's sketch. Note how it ends: "Then they [the shades, or 'Shrouds,' as the poem intriguingly renames them] began to sing, and they did not sing like men and women, but like linnets that had been stood on a perch and taught by a good singing master." The poem of course puts it far more beautifully:

They sang, but had nor human tunes nor words,
Though all was done in common as before;

They had changed their throats and had the throats of birds.

But in ending on a change from human song to birdlike song, the poem closes, conceptually, as the sketch had closed. Yeats, that is to say, knew the essence of his poem's destination before embarking on its execution proper.

I point this out because if many poets look down on the planning of a poem, they downright abhor the planning of a poem's ending. Frost, for one, couldn't have been more emphatic on the point. He says that it's "but a trick poem and no poem at all if the best of it was thought of first and saved for the last." A poem, rather, must be "a revelation, or a series of revelations, as much for the poet as for the reader." A. R. Ammons echoes Frost in saying that a poet should "be surprised by the end of the poem as much as you expect the reader to be surprised." James Merrill gives this view a personal twist in saying he finds it too *boring* to know his poems' conclusions ahead of time. (Leave it to Larkin to be a contrarian on this. He says that if he doesn't know how a poem-in-progress ends by a third of the way into it, he'll toss it.)

I'll risk opprobrium, not to say hellfire, and admit that the endings of my poems often *are* "thought of first," particularly formal poems, in which the constraints of meter and rhyme can make a good ending even harder to come by than usual. I find that I can improve my odds in this respect by writing a formal poem's ending first and letting the form of this ending help determine the form of the poem as a whole. I might add, contrary to Frost, that absent manuscript or other documentary evidence—for example, Robert Lowell's saying he wrote one of his best poems, "Skunk Hour," backward, from last stanza to first—there's no way anyone but the poet can know when in a poem's development its ending was come upon. And why would that pragmatist the reader care when? What's salient about an ending is its impact, not its history. (This isn't the place to argue for the importance of a poem's ending, though if I were going to, I'd cite John Donne's assertion in his *Sermons* that "the force of the whole piece, is for the most part left to the shutting up; the whole frame of the Poem is a beating out of a piece of gold, but the last clause is as the impression of the stamp.")

Aspiring poets are often told to "let the poem tell you where it wants to go." I'm all ears for the opinions of a poem of mine as to its path, its ending included, but not to the point where I'm willing to discount my own thoughts on the matter. When it comes to determining where a poem should go, it seems to me that poem and poet should talk things over. The give-and-take I'm envisioning might be compared to the negotiations between a dog and its walker. Poem and pooch alike should be allowed to poke their nose into things, but both are on a leash for a reason, and both are better off, for all that they may balk at times, for being guided by a master.

I sometimes find myself thinking of a poem's path in the larger context of any poem's eons-long journey toward being. A poem-to-be descends through a series of progressively smaller habitations: from universe (one of many?) to galaxy, sun, planet, poet. . . . At each step in this descent, alternatives less conducive to the poem's coming-to-be go spiraling off to their own fates. The trajectory of a poem toward its poet describes, in this sense, a kind of via negativa, a path defined by branches not gone down. This winnowing of ways continues in the poet's *inner* universe, where it takes the form of choices: from master choices of subject (should the poem have one) and treatment thereof, downward through ever more local choices from among the innumerable thoughts, phrases, and words that suggest themselves in the course of execution. Wouldn't it be a shame if, in the last few yards of this inconceivably long skein of natural and human selection, a poem were to be led offtrack by what Frost called "chance suggestions"? Yet if a poet has a proper fix on a poem's destination (that is, not *too* good a fix), chance suggestions, far from being a threat, can be a boon in infusing the poem with richness and complexity and surprise, even as the precious cargo at the poem's heart is borne, however meanderingly, toward those for whom it was meant from the beginning.

Frost, Ammons, Merrill . . . these authorities and more might say I've got this dead wrong, that the paths worth taking in poetry are precisely those one travels adventitiously. I could push back a bit by saying that even poets who emphasize spontaneity in composition tend to leave at least a little room in their emphasis for something anterior. I've already mentioned the "hunch" that Paterson says precedes his execution of a poem. Richard Hugo's ideal praxis incorporates an "initiating," or "triggering," subject that gets a poem started (if only to be leapt away from to what he calls the poem's "real" subject). Even Frost, for whom a poem is ideally a "series of revelations" for the writer as well as the reader, makes it clear that his own poems don't come out of an utter nowhere. He opens the door a crack in this regard by saying that they begin with "a lump in the throat; a homesickness or a love sickness." He opens this door markedly wider when he says that his poems begin with his "remembering something I didn't know I knew"—the operative word, for present purposes, being *something.* In an "achieved" poem, he summarizes, "an emotion has found its thought and the thought has found words."

But really, is the advisability of letting a poem "tell you where it wants to go" something one can argue, much less prove, one way or the other? When I hear Hugo say (in precise opposition to Frost) that "your words will generate your meanings," part of me feels like that 1920s-type mobster on a backward planet who's told by Captain Kirk that an armed starship is orbiting overhead. The mob guy's response—"That's *your* story, buster"—is up there with Ring Lardner's immortal "'Shut up,' he explained." The view that an author's guidance needn't hurt a poem, and in fact can help it, lends itself more to asserting than explaining. I'm well aware that anyone who asserts it is putting in a word for agency—this at a time when the very notion of "agent" is being widely called into question. (When John Ashbery was asked his opinion on something or other, he could have been speaking for many when he responded, "How should I know? I don't exist.") Yet as I suggested earlier, even if the self is an illusion, it's an illusion with consequences. The illusion called a poet has consequences called poems. At some point, the poet, like any artist—like any person—has to stop weighing alternatives and put his or her chips on a square. I'm betting that my poems are best left only so much to their own devices; that if I have at least a modest say in mapping their path, they have a better chance of delivering on their subjects' potential.

INDEX

injunction, 47-49

"In the Moonlight" (Hardy), 37-40, 85, 126

invective address, 35-37

"Irish Airman Foresees His Death, An" (Yeats), 54-56, 85

irony: Bishop's "Visits to Saint Elizabeths," 89; Browning's "To Edward Fitzgerald," 36-37; Frost's "'Out, Out—,'" 47; Hardy's "In the Moonlight," 38-39; Hughes's "Let America Be America Again," 108; Larkin's "Talking in Bed," 52

"Isn't That the Way" (Brown), 123-24

James, Henry, 122-23, 128

Jarrell, Randall, 27, 56, 77

"Jenny Kiss'd Me" (Hunt), 43, 85

journeying poems, 1-2, 70

Joyce, James: *Ulysses*, 104

Kafka, Franz: "The Bucket Rider," 70

Keats, John: address in odes of, 28; "Ode on a Grecian Urn," 17-18; "Ode to a Nightingale," 89; "On First Looking into Chapman's Homer," 21-24, 35, 84; on poetry that "has a palpable design upon us," 12

Kirby, David: "Dogs Who Are Poets and Movie Stars," 73-75; on portraying the mind, 73

Language poetry, 66-67, 103

Larkin, Philip: on endings, 132; language use, 77; "Lines on a Young Lady's Photograph Album," 91; "The Old Fools," 96; "Talking in Bed," 51-53, 85; "Toads," 110; voice of, 90-92

"Leda and the Swan" (Yeats), 20-21

"Let America Be America Again" (Hughes), 108-9

Lewitt, Sol, 103

"Lines on a Young Lady's Photograph Album" (Larkin), 91

list poetry, 69-70

"Little Gidding" (Eliot), 78

"Love a Life can show Below, The" (Dickinson), 26-28, 87, 89, 98

love poems as address, 56-59

Lowell, Robert: "Skunk Hour," 132; "'To Speak of Woe That Is in Marriage,'" 106

Machiavelli, Niccolò, 106

MacLeish, Archibald, 83

Mallarmé, Stéphane, 83

"Man and Echo, The" (Yeats), 130

Mao Tse-tung, 68

Marvell, Andrew, 83-84

McClatchy, J. D., 93

meditations: address and, 53-56; coherence and, 70-75; power and, 79-80

Mehigan, Joshua, 65

Mendelssohn, Felix, 95

Merrill, James: "Christmas Tree," 86; McClatchy on, 93; on planning, 132, 133

Merwin, W. S.: "deep image" poetry and, 104; "For the Anniversary of My Death," 82-83, 84, 104, 111; variety and, 81-82

meter: Dickinson's "Success is counted sweetest" (#112), 51; endings and, 132; Frost on sounding different and, 64; Hardy's "In the Moonlight," 39; Hayden's "Those Winter Sundays," 15; Herbert's "Prayer (I)," 26; Herbert's "The Collar," 87; Herrick's "To the Virgins to Make Much of Time," 48; Hopkins's "Thou art indeed just, Lord, if I contend," 5-6; Paterson on, 117; Pound on breaking, 83; shaped poems and, 80; Tennyson's "The Eagle," 11; Thomas's "Adlestrop," 19; Whitman's *Song of Myself*, 87

Printed in the USA
CPSIA information can be obtained
at www.ICGtesting.com
LVHW050302101123
763529LV00004B/706